FIA

FMA

ACCA

PAPER F2

MANAGEMENT ACCOUNTING

Note
From December 2011 FIA *FMA* and ACCA *Paper F2* will be examined under the same syllabus and study guide.

FOR EXAMS FROM DECEMBER 2011 TO DECEMBER 2012

PRACTICE & REVISION KIT

First edition May 2011

ISBN 9781 4453 7313 3

e-ISBN 9781 4453 7893 0

British Library Cataloguing-in-Publication Data
A catalogue record for this book
is available from the British Library

Published by

BPP Learning Media Ltd
BPP House, Aldine Place
London W12 8AA

www.bpp.com/learningmedia

Printed in the United Kingdom

Your learning materials, published by BPP
Learning Media Ltd, are printed on paper sourced
from sustainable, managed forests.

We are grateful to the Association of Chartered
Certified Accountants for permission to reproduce
past examination questions. The suggested
solutions in the exam answer bank have been
prepared by BPP Learning Media Ltd, except
where otherwise stated.

Contents

Question index

Helping you with your revision – the ONLY FMA/F2 Practice and Revision Kit to be reviewed by the examiner!

BPP Learning Media – the sole Platinum Approved Learning Partner - content

As ACCA's **sole Platinum Approved Learning Partner – content**, BPP Learning Media gives you the **unique opportunity** to use **examiner-reviewed** revision materials for exams from December 2011 to December 2012. By incorporating the examiner's comments and suggestions regarding syllabus coverage, the BPP Learning Media Practice and Revision Kit provides excellent, **ACCA-approved** support for your revision.

Selecting questions

We provide signposts to help you plan your revision.

- A full **question index** listing questions that cover each part of the syllabus, so that you can locate the questions that provide practice on key topics, and see the different ways in which they might be tested

Attempting mock exams

There are two mock exams that provide practice at coping with the pressures of the exam day. We strongly recommend that you attempt them under exam conditions. **Mock exams 1** is the Pilot paper. **Mock exam 2** reflects the question styles and syllabus coverage of the exam.

Using your BPP Practice and Revision Kit

Aim of this Practice and Revision Kit

To provide the practice to help you succeed in both the paper based and computer based examinations for Paper FMA/F2 *Management Accounting.*

To pass the examination you need a thorough understanding in all areas covered by the syllabus and teaching guide.

Recommended approach

- Make sure you are able to answer questions on **everything** specified by the syllabus and teaching guide. You cannot make any assumptions about what questions may come up on your paper. The examiners aim to discourage 'question spotting'.

- Learning is an **active** process. Use the **DO YOU KNOW**? Checklists to test your knowledge and understanding of the topics covered in FMA/F2 *Management Accounting* by filling in the blank spaces. Then check your answers against the **DID YOU KNOW**? Checklists. Do not attempt any questions if you are unable to fill in any of the blanks - go back to your **BPP Interactive Text** and revise first.

- When you are revising a topic, think about the mistakes that you know that you should avoid by writing down **POSSIBLE PITFALLS** at the end of each **DO YOU KNOW**? Checklist.

- Once you have completed the checklists successfully, you should attempt the questions on that topic. Each question is worth 2 marks and carries with it a time allocation of 2.4 minutes.

- Once you have completed all of the questions in the body of this Practice & Revision Kit, you should attempt the **MOCK EXAMS** under examination conditions. Check your answers against our answers to find out how well you did.

Passing the FMA/F2 exam

For conversion arrangements from CAT to FIA and to access CAT and FIA syllabuses, visit the ACCA website.

http://www.accaglobal.com

The exam

You can take this exam as a paper-based exam or by a computer-based exam (CBE). All questions in the exam are compulsory. This means you cannot avoid any topic, but also means that you do not need to waste time in the exam deciding which questions to attempt. There are fifty MCQs in the paper based exam and a mixture of MCQs and other types of objective test question (OTQ) (for example, number entry, multiple response and multiple response matching) in the CBE. This means that the examiner is able to test most of the syllabus at each sitting, and that is what they will aim to do. So you need to have revised right across the syllabus for this exam.

Revision

This kit has been reviewed by the FMA/F2 examiner and contains the Pilot paper, so if you just worked through it to the end you would be very well prepared for the exam. It is important to tackle questions under exam conditions. Allow yourself just the number of minutes shown next to the questions in the index and don't look at the answers until you have finished. Then correct your answer and go back to the Interactive Text for any topic you are really having trouble with. Try the same question again a week later – you will be surprised how much better you are getting. Doing the questions like this will really show you what you know, and will make the exam experience less worrying.

Doing the exam

If you have honestly done your revision you can pass this exam. There are certain points which you must bear in mind:

- Read the question properly.
- Don't spend more than the allotted time on each question. If you are having trouble with a question leave it and carry on. You can come back to it at the end.

Approach to examining the syllabus

FMA/F2 is a two-hour paper. It can be taken as a paper based or a computer based examination.

The exam is structured as follows:

	No of marks
50 compulsory multiple choice questions of 2 marks each	<u>100</u>

The Computer Based Examination

Computer based examinations (CBEs) are available for the first seven FIA papers (not papers FAU, FTM or FFM), in addition to the conventional paper based examination.

Computer based examinations must be taken at an ACCA CBE Licensed Centre.

How does CBE work?

- Questions are displayed on a monitor
- Candidates enter their answer directly onto the computer
- Candidates have two hours to complete the examination
- When the candidate has completed their examination, the final percentage score is calculated and displayed on screen
- Candidates are provided with a Provisional Result Notification showing their results before leaving the examination room
- The CBE Licensed Centre uploads the results to the ACCA (as proof of the candidate's performance) within 72 hours
- Candidates can check their exam status on the ACCA website by logging into myACCA.

Benefits

- **Flexibility** as a CBE can be sat at any time.
- **Resits** can also be taken at any time and there is no restriction on the number of times a candidate can sit a CBE.
- **Instant feedback** as the computer displays the results at the end of the CBE.
- Results are notified to ACCA **within 72 hours**.

CBE question types

- Multiple choice – choose one answer from four options
- Number entry – key in a numerical response to a question
- Multiple response – select more than one response by clicking the appropriate tick boxes
- Multiple response matching – select a response to a number of related part questions by choosing one option from a number of drop down menus

See the ACCA website for further information on computer based exams.

http://www.accaglobal.com

Tackling Multiple Choice Questions

MCQs are part of all FIA exams. They form the paper based exams and may appear in the CBE.

The MCQs in your exam contain four possible answers. You have to **choose the option that best answers the question**. The three incorrect options are called distracters. There is a skill in answering MCQs quickly and correctly. By practising MCQs you can develop this skill, giving you a better chance of passing the exam.

You may wish to follow the approach outlined below, or you may prefer to adapt it.

Step 1	Skim read all the MCQs and identify what appear to be the easier questions.
Step 2	Attempt each question – **starting with the easier questions** identified in Step 1. Read the question **thoroughly**. You may prefer to work out the answer before looking at the options, or you may prefer to look at the options at the beginning. Adopt the method that works best for you.
Step 3	Read the four options and see if one matches your own answer. Be careful with numerical questions as the distracters are designed to match answers that incorporate common errors. Check that your calculation is correct. Have you followed the requirement exactly? Have you included every stage of the calculation?
Step 4	You may find that none of the options matches your answer. • Re-read the question to ensure that you understand it and are answering the requirement • Eliminate any obviously wrong answers • Consider which of the remaining answers is the most likely to be correct and select the option
Step 5	If you are still unsure make a note and continue to the next question
Step 6	Revisit unanswered questions. When you come back to a question after a break you often find you are able to answer it correctly straight away. If you are still unsure have a guess. You are not penalised for incorrect answers, so **never leave a question unanswered!**

After extensive practice and revision of MCQs, you may find that you recognise a question when you sit the exam. Be aware that the detail and/or requirement may be different. If the question seems familiar read the requirement and options carefully – do not assume that it is identical.

Using your BPP products

This Kit gives you the question practice and guidance you need in the exam. Our other products can also help you pass:

- **Passcards** provide you with clear topic summaries and exam tips

- **i-Pass CDs** are a vital revision tool for anyone taking FIA/ACCA CBEs and offer tests of knowledge against the clock in an environment similar to that encountered in a computer based exam

You can purchase these products by visiting www.bpp.com/learningmedia

Questions

Do you know? – Accounting for management

Check that you can fill in the blanks in the statements below before you attempt any questions. If in doubt, you should go back to your BPP Interactive Text and revise first.

- Good information should be ...., ..., ..., and .... It should inspire confidence, it should be appropriately communicated, its volume should be manageable, it should be timely and its cost should be less than the benefits it provides

- Information for management is likely to be used for

    – ....
    – ....
    – ....

- The main objective of profit making organisations is to .... A secondary objective of profit making organisations might be to increase .... of its goods/services.

- The main objective of non-profit making organisations is usually to .... and services. A secondary objective of non-profit making organisations might be to minimise the .... involved in providing the goods/services.

- Long-term .... planning, also known as corporate planning, involves selecting appropriate .... so as to prepare a long-term plan to attain the objectives

- Anthony divides management activities into .... planning, ... control and .... control.

- Tactical (or management) control: 'the process by which managers assure that .... are obtained and used effectively and efficiently in the accomplishment of the organisation's objectives'.

    Operational control: 'the process of assuring that specific .... are carried out .... and ....

- .... accounts are prepared for individuals external to an organisation: shareholders, customers, suppliers, tax authorities, employees.

    .... accounts are prepared for internal managers of an organisation.

- There is no legal requirement to prepare .... accounts.

- .... accounts are both an historical record and a future planning tool.

- .... accounts concentrate on the business as a whole, aggregating revenues and costs from different operations, and are an end in themselves.

- Management accounting information is, in general, unsuitable for ....

- *Possible pitfalls*

    – Write down the mistakes you know you should avoid.

Did you know? – Accounting for management

Could you fill in the blanks? The answers are in bold. Use this page for revision purposes as you approach the exam.

- Good information should be **relevant**, **complete**, **accurate**, and **clear**. It should inspire confidence, it should be appropriately communicated, its volume should be manageable, it should be timely and its cost should be less than the benefits it provides

- Information for management is likely to be used for

    – **Planning**
    – **Control**
    – **Decision-making**

- The main objective of profit making organisations is to **maximise profits**. A secondary objective of profit making organisations might be to increase **output** of its goods/services.

- The main objective of non-profit making organisations is usually to **provide goods** and **services**. A secondary objective of non-profit making organisations might be to minimise the **costs** involved in providing the goods/services.

- **Long-term strategic planning**, also known as corporate planning, involves selecting appropriate strategies so as to prepare a long-term plan to attain the objectives.

- Anthony divides management activities into **strategic** planning, **management** control and **operational** control.

- Tactical (or management) control: 'the process by which managers assure that **resources** are obtained and used effectively and efficiently in the accomplishment of the organisation's objectives'.

    Operational control: 'the process of assuring that specific **tasks** are carried out **effectively** and **efficiently**'.

- **Financial accounts** are prepared for individuals external to an organisation: shareholders, customers, suppliers, tax authorities, employees.

    Management accounts are prepared for internal managers of an organisation.

- There is no legal requirement to prepare **management** accounts.

- **Management accounts** are both an historical record and a future planning tool.

- **Financial accounts** concentrate on the business as a whole, aggregating revenues and costs from different operations, and are an end in themselves.

- Management accounting information is, in general, unsuitable for **decision making**.

- *Possible pitfalls*

    – Forgetting the differences between financial and management accounting

1 Accounting for management — 17 mins

1.1 Which of the following statements about qualities of good information is false?

A It should be relevant for its purposes
B It should be communicated to the right person
C It should be completely accurate
D It should be timely **(2 marks)**

1.2 The sales manager has prepared a manpower plan to ensure that sales quotas for the forthcoming year are achieved. This is an example of what type of planning?

A Strategic planning
B Tactical planning
C Operational planning
D Corporate planning **(2 marks)**

1.3 Which of the following statements about management accounting information is/are true?

1 They must be stated in purely monetary terms
2 Limited companies must, by law, prepare management accounts
3 They serve as a future planning tool and are not used as an historical record

A 1, 2 and 3
B 1 and 2
C 2 only
D None of the statements is true **(2 marks)**

1.4 Which of the following statements is/are correct?

1 A management control system is a term used to describe the hardware and software used to drive a database system which produces information outputs that are easily assimilated by management.

2 An objective is a course of action that an organisation might pursue in order to achieve its strategy.

3 Information is data that has been processed into a form meaningful to the recipient.

A 1, 2 and 3
B 1 and 3
C 2 and 3
D 3 only **(2 marks)**

1.5 Good information should have certain qualities. Which of the following are qualities of good information?

1 Complete
2 Extensive
3 Relevant
4 Accurate

A 1, 2 and 3
B 1, 3 and 4
C 2 and 4
D All of them **(2 marks)**

1.6 Monthly variance reports are an example of which one of the following types of management information?

    A   Tactical
    B   Strategic
    C   Non-financial
    D   Operational   **(2 marks)**

1.7 Which of the following statements is/are correct?

    1   **Strategic planning** is carried out by front-line managers.
    2   Non-financial information is relevant to management accounting.

    A   1 is true and 2 is false
    B   2 is true and 1 is false
    C   Both are true
    D   Both are false   **(2 marks)**

(Total = 14 marks)

Do you know? – Sources of data

Check that you can fill in the blanks in the statements below before you attempt any questions. If in doubt, you should go back to your BPP Interactive Text and revise first

- Data may be .... (collected specifically for the purpose of a survey) or .... (collected for some other purpose)

  You will remember that primary data are data collected especially for a specific purpose. The advantage of such data is that the investigator knows where the data .... and is aware of any inadequacies or limitations in the data. Its disadvantage is that it can be very .... to collect primary data

- Secondary data sources may be satisfactory in certain situations, or they may be the only convenient means of obtaining an item of data. It is essential that there is good reason to believe that the secondary data used is .... and ....

- The main sources of secondary data are:

  - .... - ....
  - .... - ....
  - .... - ....
  - .... - ....

- In such situations where it is not possible to survey the whole population, a .... is selected. The results obtained from this are used to estimate the results of the whole population. In situations where the whole population is examined, the survey is called a .... This situation is quite rare, which means that the investigator must choose a sample.

- A .... sampling method is a sampling method in which there is a known chance of each member of the population appearing in the sample.

- A .... sample is a sample selected in such a way that every item in the population has an equal chance of being included.

- If random sampling is used then it is necessary to construct a .... Once a numbered list of all items in the population has been made, it is easy to select a .... sample, simply by generating a list of random numbers

- .... random sampling is a method of sampling which involves dividing the population into strata or categories. Random samples are then taken from each stratum or category. The main disadvantage of stratification is that it requires .... of each item in the population; sampling frames do not always contain such information.

- Systematic sampling is a sampling method which works by selecting every nth item after a random start. The advantages of systematic sampling are .... and ....

- Multistage sampling is a probability sampling method which involves dividing the .... into a number of ....-........... and then selecting a small sample of these at random. Each .....-.......... is then divided further, and then a small sample is again selected at random. This process is repeated as many times as is necessary.

- .... sampling is a non-random sampling method that involves selecting one definable subsection of the population as the sample, that subsection taken to be representative of the population in question.

- In quota sampling, ... is forfeited in the interests of cheapness and administrative simplicity. Investigators are told to interview all the people they meet up to a certain quota.

- *Possible pitfalls*

  - Write down the mistakes you know you should avoid.

Did you know? – Sources of data

Could you fill in the blanks? The answers are in bold. Use this page for revision purposes as you approach the exam.

- Data may be **primary** (collected specifically for the purpose of a survey) or **secondary** (collected for some other purpose).

  You will remember that primary data are data collected especially for a specific purpose. The advantage of such data is that the investigator knows where the data **came from** and is aware of any inadequacies or limitations in the data. Its disadvantage is that it can be very **expensive** to collect primary data.

- Secondary data sources may be satisfactory in certain situations, or they may be the only convenient means of obtaining an item of data. It is essential that there is good reason to believe that the secondary data used is **accurate** and **reliable**

- The main sources of secondary data are: **Governments; banks; newspapers; trade journals; information bureaux; consultancies; libraries and information services**.

- In such situations where it is not possible to survey the whole population, a **sample** is selected. The results obtained from this are used to estimate the results of the whole population. In situations where the whole population is examined, the survey is called a **census**. This situation is quite rare, which means that the investigator must choose a sample.

- A **probability** sampling method is a sampling method in which there is a known chance of each member of the population appearing in the sample.

- A **simple random** sample is a sample selected in such a way that every item in the population has an equal chance of being included..

- If random sampling is used then it is necessary to construct a **sampling frame**. Once a numbered list of all items in the population has been made, it is easy to select a **random** sample, simply by generating a list of random numbers.

- **Stratified** random sampling is a method of sampling which involves dividing the population into strata or categories. Random samples are then taken from each stratum or category. The main disadvantage of stratification is that it requires **prior knowledge** of each item in the population; sampling frames do not always contain such information.

- Systematic sampling is a sampling method which works by selecting every nth item after a random start. The advantages of systematic sampling are

  It is easy to use.
  It is cheap.

- Multistage sampling is a probability sampling method which involves dividing the **population** into a number of **sub-populations** and then selecting a small sample of these at random. Each **sub-population** is then divided further, and then a small sample is again selected at random. This process is repeated as many times as is necessary.

- **Cluster** sampling is a non-random sampling method that involves selecting one definable subsection of the population as the sample, that subsection taken to be representative of the population in question.

- In quota sampling, **randomness** is forfeited in the interests of cheapness and administrative simplicity. Investigators are told to interview all the people they meet up to a certain quota.

- *Possible pitfalls*

  - Mixing up the different types of sampling
  - Not knowing the advantages and disadvantages of the sampling methods

2 Sources of data   12 mins

2.1   Which of the following is/are primary sources of data?

  (i)   Historical records of transport costs to be used to prepare forecasts for budgetary planning

  (ii)   The *Annual Abstract of Statistics*, published by the Office for National Statistics in the United Kingdom

  (iii) Data collected by a bank in a telephone survey to monitor the effectiveness of the bank's customer services

  A   (i) and (ii)
  B   (i) and (iii)
  C   (i) only
  D   (iii) only   **(2 marks)**

2.2   The following statements relate to different types of data

  (i)   Secondary data are data collected especially for a specific purpose
  (ii)   Discrete data can take on any value
  (iii) Qualitative data are data that cannot be measured
  (iv)   Population data are data arising as a result of investigating a group of people or objects

  Which of the statements are true?

  A   (i) and (ii) only
  B   (ii) and (iii) only
  C   (ii) and (iv) only
  D   (iii) and (iv) only   **(2 marks)**

2.3   Which of the following statements are not true?

  I   If a sample is selected using random sampling, it will be free from bias.

  II   A sampling frame is a numbered list of all items in a sample.

  III   In cluster sampling there is very little potential for bias.

  IV   In quota sampling, investigators are told to interview all the people they meet up to a certain quota.

  A   I, II, III and IV
  B   I, II and III
  C   II and III
  D   II only   **(2 marks)**

2.4   Which of the following sampling methods require a sampling frame?

  (i)   Random
  (ii)   Stratified
  (iii) Quota
  (iv)   Systematic

  A   (i) and (ii) only
  B   (i), (ii) and (iii) only
  C   (i), (ii) and (iv) only
  D   (iii) only   **(2 marks)**

2.5   Which of the following explains the essence of quota sampling?

  A   Each element of the population has an equal chance of being chosen
  B   Every nth member of the population is selected
  C   Every element of one definable sub-section of the population is selected
  D   None of the above   **(2 marks)**

                                                            (Total = 10 marks)

Do you know? – Cost classification and cost behaviour

Check that you can fill in the blanks in the statements below before you attempt any questions. If in doubt, you should go back to your BPP Interactive Text and revise first.

- A .... cost is a cost that can be traced in full to the product, service or department that is being costed. An .... cost is a cost that is incurred in the course of making a product, providing a service or running a department but which cannot be traced directly and in full to the product, service or department.

- In classification by function, costs are classified as follows

    – .... These are associated with the factory

    – .... These are costs associated with general office departments

    – .... These are costs associated with sales, marketing, warehousing and transport departments

- A .... cost is a cost which is incurred for a particular period of time and which, within certain activity levels, is unaffected by changes in the level of activity. A .... cost is a cost which tends to vary with the level of activity. Many items of expenditure are part .... and part .... and are called .... costs.

- The distinction between production and non-production costs is the basis of valuing ....

- A .... centre is a department or organisational function whose performance is the direct responsibility of a specific manager.

    .... centres are similar to cost centres but are accountable for costs and revenues.

    An .... centre is a profit centre with additional responsibilities for capital investment and possibly for financing, and whose performance is measured by its return on investment.

- The basic principle of cost behaviour is that as the level of activity rises, costs will usually ....

- The effect of increasing activity levels on unit costs is as follows. (Tick as appropriate)

	Rises	Falls	Remains constant
Variable cost per unit			
Fixed cost per unit			
Total cost per unit			

- The fixed and variable elements of semi-variable costs can be determined by the .... method.

- *Possible pitfalls*

    – Write down the mistakes you know you should avoid.

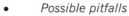

Did you know? – Cost classification and cost behaviour

Could you fill in the blanks? The answers are in bold. Use this page for revision purposes as you approach the exam.

- A **direct** cost is a cost that can be traced in full to the product, service or department that is being costed. An **indirect** cost is a cost that is incurred in the course of making a product, providing a service or running a department but which cannot be traced directly and in full to the product, service or department.

- In classification by function, costs are classified as follows

  - **Production or manufacturing costs**. These are associated with the factory

  - **Administration costs**. These are costs associated with general office departments

  - **Marketing or selling and distribution costs**. These are costs associated with sales, marketing, warehousing and transport departments

- A **fixed** cost is a cost which is incurred for a particular period of time and which, within certain activity levels, is unaffected by changes in the level of activity. A **variable** cost is a cost which tends to vary with the level of activity. Many items of expenditure are part **fixed** and part **variable** and are called **semi-variable** costs.

- The distinction between production and non-production costs is the basis of valuing **inventory**

- A **responsibility** centre is a department or organisational function whose performance is the direct responsibility of a specific manager.

  Profit centres are similar to cost centres but are accountable for costs and revenues.

- An **investment** centre is a profit centre with additional responsibilities for capital investment and possibly for financing, and whose performance is measured by its return on investment.

- The basic principle of cost behaviour is that as the level of activity rises, costs will usually **rise**.

- The effect of changing activity levels on unit costs is as follows. (Tick as appropriate)

	Rises	Falls	Remains constant
Variable cost per unit			✓
Fixed cost per unit		✓	
Total cost per unit		✓	

- The fixed and variable elements of semi-variable costs can be determined by the **high-low** method.

- *Possible pitfalls*

  - Getting confused between fixed and variable costs – particularly if they are expressed per unit.
  - Not grasping the difference between direct and indirect costs.

3 Cost classification   26 mins

3.1   A firm has to pay a 20c per unit royalty to the inventor of a device which it manufactures and sells.

How would the royalty charge be classified in the firm's accounts?

    A   Selling expense
    B   Direct expense
    C   Production overhead
    D   Administrative overhead   **(2 marks)**

3.2   Which of the following would be classed as indirect labour?

    A   Assembly workers in a company manufacturing televisions
    B   A stores assistant in a factory store
    C   Plasterers in a construction company
    D   A consultant in a firm of management consultants   **(2 marks)**

3.3   A manufacturing firm is very busy and overtime is being worked.

How would the amount of overtime premium contained in direct wages normally be classed?

    A   Part of prime cost
    B   Factory overheads
    C   Direct labour costs
    D   Administrative overheads   **(2 marks)**

3.4   Which of the following items would be treated as an indirect cost?

    A   Wood used to make a chair
    B   Metal used for the legs of a chair
    C   Fabric to cover the seat of a chair
    D   Staples to fix the fabric to the seat of a chair   **(2 marks)**

3.5   Over which of the following is the manager of a profit centre likely to have control?

    (i)   Selling prices
    (ii)   Controllable costs
    (iii)   Apportioned head office costs
    (iv)   Capital investment in the centre

    A   All of the above
    B   (i), (ii) and (iii)
    C   (i), (ii) and (iv)
    D   (i) and (ii)   **(2 marks)**

3.6   Which of the following best describes a controllable cost?

    A   A cost which arises from a decision already taken, which cannot, in the short run, be changed.

    B   A cost for which the behaviour pattern can be easily analysed to facilitate valid budgetary control comparisons.

    C   A cost which can be influenced by its budget holder.

    D   A specific cost of an activity or business which would be avoided if the activity or business did not exist.   **(2 marks)**

3.7 Which of the following items might be a suitable cost unit within the credit control department of a company?

    (i)   Stationery cost
    (ii)   Customer account
    (iii)   Cheque received and processed

    A   Item (i) only
    B   Item (ii) only
    C   Item (iii) only
    D   Items (ii) and (iii) only   **(2 marks)**

3.8 Which of the following best describes a period cost?

    A   A cost that relates to a time period which is deducted as expenses for the period and is not included in the inventory valuation.

    B   A cost that can be easily allocated to a particular period, without the need for arbitrary apportionment between periods.

    C   A cost that is identified with a unit produced during the period, and is included in the value of inventory. The cost is treated as an expense for the period when the inventory is actually sold.

    D   A cost that is incurred regularly every period, eg every month or quarter.   **(2 marks)**

3.9 A company employs four supervisors to oversee the factory production of all its products. How would the salaries paid to these supervisors be classified?

    A   As a direct labour cost
    B   As a direct production expense
    C   As a production overhead
    D   As an administration overhead   **(2 marks)**

3.10 A company manufactures and sells toys and incurs the following three costs:

    (i)   Rental of the finished goods warehouse
    (ii)   Depreciation of its own fleet of delivery vehicles
    (iii)   Commission paid to sales staff

Which of these are classified as distribution costs?

    A   (i) and (ii) only
    B   (i) and (iii) only
    C   (ii) and (iii) only
    D   (i), (ii) and (iii)   **(2 marks)**

3.11 Which of the following describes a cost centre?

    A   A unit of output or service for which costs are ascertained
    B   A function or location for which costs are ascertained
    C   A segment of the organisation for which budgets are prepared
    D   An amount of expenditure attributable to a particular activity   **(2 marks)**

(Total = 22 marks)

4 Cost behaviour   46 mins

4.1 Fixed costs are conventionally deemed to be:

    A   Constant per unit of output
    B   Constant in total when production volume changes
    C   Outside the control of management
    D   Easily controlled   **(2 marks)**

4.2   The following data relate to the overhead expenditure of a contract cleaners at two activity levels.

Square metres cleaned   13,500   15,950

Overheads $84,865 $97,850

What is the estimate of the overheads if 18,300 square metres are to be cleaned?

    A $96,990
    B $110,305
    C $112,267
    D $115,039   **(2 marks)**

The following information relates to questions 4.3 to 4.7

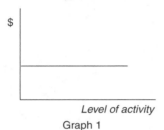

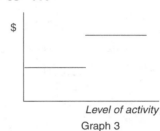

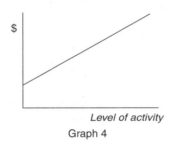

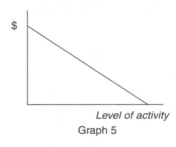

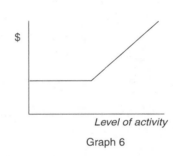

Which one of the above graphs illustrates the costs described in questions 4.3 to 4.7?

4.3   A linear variable cost – when the vertical axis represents cost incurred.

    A   Graph 1
    B   Graph 2
    C   Graph 4
    D   Graph 5   **(2 marks)**

4.4   A fixed cost – when the vertical axis represents cost incurred.

    A   Graph 1
    B   Graph 2
    C   Graph 3
    D   Graph 6   **(2 marks)**

4.5   A linear variable cost – when the vertical axis represents cost per unit.

    A   Graph 1
    B   Graph 2
    C   Graph 3
    D   Graph 6   **(2 marks)**

4.6   A semi-variable cost – when the vertical axis represents cost incurred.

    A   Graph 1
    B   Graph 2
    C   Graph 4
    D   Graph 5   **(2 marks)**

4.7 A step fixed cost – when the vertical axis represents cost incurred.

    A   Graph 3
    B   Graph 4
    C   Graph 5
    D   Graph 6   **(2 marks)**

4.8 A company has recorded the following data in the two most recent periods.

Total costs of production $	Volume of production Units
13,500	700
18,300	1,100

What is the best estimate of the company's fixed costs per period?

    A $13,500
    B $13,200
    C $5,100
    D $4,800   **(2 marks)**

4.9 A production worker is paid a salary of $650 per month, plus an extra 5 pence for each unit produced during the month. How is this type of labour cost best described?

    A   A variable cost
    B   A fixed cost
    C   A step cost
    D   A semi-variable cost   **(2 marks)**

4.10 What type of cost is supervisor salary costs, where one supervisor is needed for every ten employees added to the staff?

    A   A fixed cost
    B   A variable cost
    C   A mixed cost
    D   A step cost   **(2 marks)**

4.11 The following information for advertising and sales has been established over the past six months:

Month	Sales revenue $'000	Advertising expenditure $'000
1	155	3
2	125	2.5
3	200	6
4	175	5.5
5	150	4.5
6	225	6.5

Using the high-low method which of the following is the correct equation for linking advertising and sales from the above data?

    A   Sales revenue = 62,500 + (25 × advertising expenditure)
    B   Advertising expenditure = – 2,500 + (0.04 × sales revenue)
    C   Sales revenue = 95,000 + (20 × advertising expenditure)
    D   Advertising expenditure = – 4,750 + (0.05 × sales revenue)   **(2 marks)**

4.12 A total cost is described as staying the same over a certain activity range and then increasing but remaining stable over a revised activity range in the short term.

What type of cost is this?

A   A fixed cost
B   A variable cost
C   A semi-variable cost
D   A stepped fixed cost   **(2 marks)**

4.13 A company incurs the following costs at various activity levels:

Total cost	Activity level
$	units
250,000	5,000
312,500	7,500
400,000	10,000

Using the high-low method what is the variable cost per unit?

A $25
B $30
C $35
D $40   **(2 marks)**

4.14 The following diagram represents the behaviour of one element of cost:

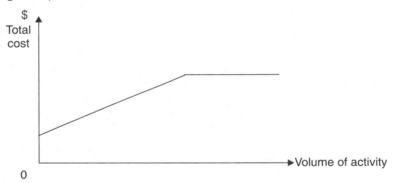

Which ONE of the following statements is consistent with the above diagram?

A   Annual factory power cost where the electricity supplier sets a tariff based on a fixed charge plus a constant unit cost for consumption but subject to a maximum annual charge.

B   Weekly total labour cost when there is a fixed wage for a standard 40 hour week but overtime is paid at a premium rate.

C   Total direct material cost for a period if the supplier charges a lower unit cost on all units once a certain quantity has been purchased in that period.

D   Total direct material cost for a period where the supplier charges a constant amount per unit for all units supplied up to a maximum charge for the period.   **(2 marks)**

4.15 An organisation manufactures a single product. The total cost of making 4,000 units is $20,000 and the total cost of making 20,000 units is $40,000. Within this range of activity the total fixed costs remain unchanged.

What is the variable cost per unit of the product?

A $0.80
B $1.20
C $1.25
D $2.00   **(2 marks)**

4.16 When total purchases of raw material exceed 30,000 units in any one period then all units purchased, including the initial 30,000, are invoiced at a lower cost per unit.

Which of the following graphs is consistent with the behaviour of the total materials cost in a period?

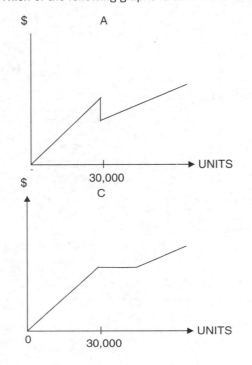
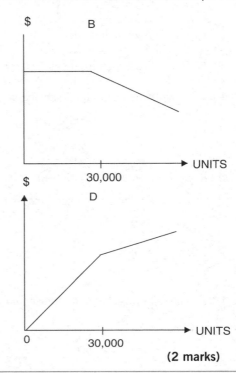

(2 marks)

4.17 The total cost of production for two levels of activity is as follows:

	Level 1	Level 2
Production (units)	3,000	5,000
Total cost ($)	6,750	9,250

The variable production cost per unit and the total fixed production cost both remain constant in the range of activity shown.

What is the level of fixed costs?

A $2,000   C $3,000
B $2,500   D $3,500   (2 marks)

4.18 The following data relate to two activity levels of an X-ray department in a hospital:

Number of X-rays taken	4,500	4,750
Overheads	$269,750	$273,625

Fixed overheads are $200,000 per period.

What is the variable cost per X-ray?

A $0.06   C $250
B $15.50   D $3,875   (2 marks)

4.19 An organisation has found that there is a linear relationship between sales volume and delivery costs.

It has found that a sales volume of 400 units corresponds to delivery costs of $10,000 and that a sales volume of 800 units corresponds to delivery costs of $12,000.

What are the delivery costs for a sales volume of 700 units?

A $5   C $8,000
B $3,500   D $11,500   (2 marks)

(Total = 38 marks)

5 Presenting information   7 mins

5.1   The cost of materials for product A are as follows.

Material W: $2,250
Material X: $3,000
Material Y: $3,600
Material Z: $150

If the material proportions were displayed on a pie chart, how many degrees would material Y represent?

A	90 degrees	C	144 degrees
B	120 degrees	D	204 degrees

(2 marks)

The following information relates to questions 5.2 to 5.3

	Number of ice-creams sold			
	April	May	June	July
Mint choc chip	600	760	725	900
Chocolate	300	335	360	525
Strawberry	175	260	310	475
Blueberry	75	90	100	90

5.2   The data may be illustrated by the following chart. What type of chart is it?

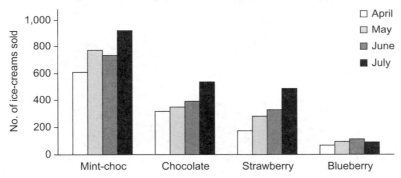

A   Simple bar chart
B   Multiple bar chart
C   Component bar chart
D   Ogive   **(2 marks)**

5.3   Which one of the following statements is true?

A   Sales of mint choc chip rose steadily over the four months
B   Total sales fell in the month of July
C   After May, sales of strawberry began to catch up with sales of chocolate
D   Sales of blueberry rose in May and July   **(2 marks)**

(Total = 6 marks)

Do you know? – Materials and labour

Check that you can fill in the blanks in the statements below before you attempt any questions. If in doubt, you should go back to your BPP Interactive Text and revise first.

- FIFO prices materials issues at the prices of the newest/oldest items in inventory, and values closing inventory at the value of the most recent/oldest items in inventory. (Delete as appropriate)

- LIFO prices materials issues at the prices of the newest/oldest items in inventory and values closing inventory at the value of the most recent/oldest items. (Delete as appropriate)

- ....is usually carried out annually, when all items of inventory are counted on a specific date. .... involves counting and checking a number of inventory items on a regular basis so that each item is checked at least once a year.

- Inventory control levels are calculated in order to maintain inventory at the optimum level. The four critical control levels are as follows.

  .... (maximum usage × maximum lead time)
  .... (quantity of inventory to be reordered when inventory reaches reorder level)
  .... (reorder level – (average usage × average lead time))
  .... (reorder level + reorder quantity – (min usage × min lead time))

- The .... is the ordering quantity which minimises inventory costs (holding costs and ordering costs), and is calculated as follows.

  $$EOQ = \sqrt{\frac{2C_0D}{C_h}}$$ Where C_h = ...

  C_o = ...
  D = ...
  EOQ = ...

- Labour attendance time is recorded on an .... or on a .... Job time is recorded on the following documents:

  ....
  ....
  ....
  ....

- The labour cost of work done by pieceworkers is recorded on a .... (operation card). Piecework, time-saved bonus, discretionary bonus, group bonus scheme and profit-sharing are all different types of .... scheme.

- *Possible pitfalls*

  Write down the mistakes you know you should avoid.

Did you know? – Materials and labour

Could you fill in the blanks? The answers are in bold. Use this page for revision purposes as you approach the exam.

- FIFO prices materials issues at the prices of the ~~newest~~/**oldest** items in inventory, and values closing inventory at the value of the **most recent**/~~oldest~~ items in inventory.

- LIFO prices materials issues at the prices of the **newest**/~~oldest~~ items in inventory and values closing inventory at the value of the most ~~recent~~/**oldest items**.

- **Periodic inventory taking** is usually carried out annually, when all items of inventory are counted on a specific date. **Continuous inventory taking** involves counting and checking a number of inventory items on a regular basis so that each item is checked at least once a year.

- Inventory control levels are calculated in order to maintain inventory at the optimum level. The four critical control levels are as follows.

  Reorder level (maximum usage × maximum lead time)
  Reorder quantity (quantity of inventory to be reordered when inventory reaches reorder level)
  Minimum inventory level (reorder level – (average usage × average lead time))
  Maximum inventory level (reorder level + reorder quantity – (min usage × min lead time))

- The **economic order quantity** is the ordering quantity which minimises inventory costs (holding costs and ordering costs), and is calculated as follows.

  $$EOQ = \sqrt{\frac{2C_0 D}{C_h}}$$

  Where C_h = **holding costs of one unit of inventory for one year**

             Co   = **cost of ordering a consignment**
             D   = **annual demand**
             EOQ   = **economic order quantity**

- Labour attendance time is recorded on an **attendance card** or on a **clock card.** Job time is recorded on the following documents.

  Daily time sheets
  Weekly time sheets
  Job cards
  Route cards

- The labour cost of work done by pieceworkers is recorded on a **piecework ticket** (operation card). Piecework, time-saved bonus, discretionary bonus, group bonus scheme and profit-sharing are all different types of **incentive** scheme.

- *Possible pitfalls*

  Confusing FIFO with LIFO
  Not being able to reproduce the inventory control formulae
  Confusing the meaning of 'c', 'd', and 'h' in the economic order quantity equation

6 Material costs   41 mins

6.1   Which of the following functions are fulfilled by a goods received note (GRN)?

      (i)   Provides information to update the inventory records on receipt of goods
      (ii)   Provides information to check the quantity on the supplier's invoice
      (iii) Provides information to check the price on the supplier's invoice

      A   (i) and (ii) only
      B   (i) and (iii) only
      C   (ii) and (iii) only
      D   (i) only   **(2 marks)**

6.2   There are 27,500 units of Part Number X35 on order with the suppliers and 16,250 units outstanding
      on existing customers' orders.

      If the free inventory is 13,000 units, what is the physical inventory?

      A   1,750
      B   3,250
      C   24,250
      D   29,250   **(2 marks)**

The following information relates to questions 6.3 and 6.4

A domestic appliance retailer with multiple outlets sells a popular toaster known as the Autocrisp 2000, for
which the following information is available:

Average sales	75 per day
Maximum sales	95 per day
Minimum sales	50 per day
Lead time	12-18 days
Reorder quantity	1,750

6.3   Based on the data above, at what level of inventory would a replenishment order be issued?

      A   600 units
      B   1,125 units
      C   1,710 units
      D   1,750 units   **(2 marks)**

6.4   Based on the data above, what is the maximum inventory level?

      A   1,750 units
      B   2,275 units
      C   2,860 units
      D   2,900 units   **(2 marks)**

6.5   The annual demand for an item of inventory is 2,500 units. The cost of placing an order is $80 and the
      cost of holding an item in stock for one year is $15. What is the economic order quantity, to the nearest
      unit?

      A   31 units
      B   115 units
      C   163 units
      D   26,667 units   **(2 marks)**

6.6   Which of the following is correct with regard to inventories?

(i)   Stock-outs arise when too little inventory is held

(ii)   Safety inventories are the level of units maintained in case there is unexpected demand

(iii)   A re-order level can be established by looking at the maximum usage and the maximum lead-time

A   (i) and (ii) only
B   (i) and (iii) only
C   (ii) and (iii) only
D   (i), (ii) and (iii)   **(2 marks)**

6.7   What is the economic batch quantity used to establish?

Optimal

A   reorder quantity
B   recorder level
C   cumulative production quantity
D   inventory level for production   **(2 marks)**

6.8   The demand for a product is 12,500 units for a three month period. Each unit of product has a purchase price of $15 and ordering costs are $20 per order placed.

The annual holding cost of one unit of product is 10% of its purchase price.

What is the Economic Order Quantity (to the nearest unit)?

A   577
B   816
C   866
D   1,155   **(2 marks)**

6.9   A company determines its order quantity for a raw material by using the Economic Order Quantity (EOQ) model.

What would be the effects on the EOQ and the total annual holding cost of a decrease in the cost of ordering a batch of raw material?

	EOQ	Total annual holding cost
A	Higher	Lower
B	Higher	Higher
C	Lower	Higher
D	Lower	Lower

(2 marks)

6.10   Data relating to a particular stores item are as follows:

Average daily usage	400 units
Maximum daily usage	520 units
Minimum daily usage	180 units
Lead time for replenishment of inventory	10 to 15 days
Reorder quantity	8,000 units

What is the reorder level (in units) which avoids stockouts (running out of inventory)?

A   5,000
B   6,000
C   7,800
D   8,000   **(2 marks)**

6.11 The material stores control account for a company for March looks like this:

MATERIAL STORES CONTROL ACCOUNT

	$		$
Balance b/d	12,000	Work in progress	40,000
Suppliers	49,000	Overhead control	12,000
Work in progress	18,000	Balance c/d	27,000
	79,000		79,000
Balance b/d	27,000		

Which of the following statements are correct?

(i)   Issues of direct materials during March were $18,000
(ii)   Issues of direct materials during March were $40,000
(iii)   Issues of indirect materials during March were $12,000
(iv)   Purchases of materials during March were $49,000

A   (i) and (iv) only
B   (ii) and (iv) only
C   (ii), (iii) and (iv) only
D   All of them   **(2 marks)**

6.12 A manufacturing company uses 25,000 components at an even rate during a year. Each order placed with the supplier of the components is for 2,000 components, which is the economic order quantity. The company holds a buffer inventory of 500 components. The annual cost of holding one component in inventory is $2.

What is the total annual cost of holding inventory of the component?

A $2,000
B $2,500
C $3,000
D $4,000   **(2 marks)**

6.13 A company wishes to minimise its inventory costs. Order costs are $10 per order and holding costs are $0.10 per unit per month. Fall Co estimates annual demand to be 5,400 units.

The economic order quantity is ⌷ units.

A   949
B   90,000
C   1,039
D   300   **(2 marks)**

6.14 For a particular component, the re-order quantity is 6,000 units and the average inventory holding is 3,400 units.

The level of safety inventory is (in whole units)

A   400
B   3,400
C   3,000
D   6,400   **(2 marks)**

6.15 The following data relates to component L512:

Ordering costs $100 per order
Inventory holding costs $8 per unit per annum
Annual demand   1,225 units

The economic order quantity is ☐ units (to the nearest whole unit)

A   175
B   62
C   44
D   124   **(2 marks)**

6.16 The following data relate to inventory item A452:

Average usage	100 units per day
Minimum usage	60 units per day
Maximum usage	130 units per day
Lead time	20-26 days
EOQ	4,000 units

The maximum inventory level was ☐ units

A   3,380
B   6,180
C   7,380
D   8,580   **(2 marks)**

6.17 ACB Co gradually receives its re-supply of inventory at a rate of 10,000 units a week. Other information is available as follows.

Weekly demand	5,000 units
Set-up costs for each production run	$125
Weekly cost of holding one unit	$0.0025

What is the economic production run?

A   1,577 units
B   7,071 units
C   31,623 units
D   894,427 units   **(2 marks)**

(Total = 34 marks)

7 Labour   26 mins

The following information relates to questions 7.1 and 7.2

Budgeted and actual production data for the year that has just ended are as follows.

Product	Budgeted production		Actual production
	Units	Standard machine hours	Units
W	15,000	3,000	12,000
X	20,000	8,000	25,000
Y	14,000	7,000	16,000
Z	6,000	9,000	5,000

Total machine hours worked in the period amounted to 29,000 hours.

7.1 What was the capacity ratio in the year, as a percentage to one decimal place?

A 93.1%
B 103.3%
C 105.5%
D 107.4%   **(2 marks)**

7.2 What was the efficiency ratio in the year, as a percentage to one decimal place?

A 96.2%
B 103.3%
C 103.9%
D 107.4%   **(2 marks)**

7.3 The labour cost graph below depicts:

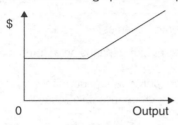

A A piece rate scheme with a minimum guaranteed wage
B A straight piece rate scheme
C A straight time rate scheme
D A differential piece rate scheme   **(2 marks)**

7.4 The following data relate to work in the finishing department of a certain factory.

Normal working day	7 hours
Basic rate of pay per hour	$5
Standard time allowed to produce 1 unit	4 minutes
Premium bonus payable at the basic rate	60% of time saved

On a particular day one employee finishes 180 units. His gross pay for the day will be

A $35
B $50
C $56
D $60   **(2 marks)**

7.5 An employee is paid on a piecework basis. The basis of the piecework scheme is as follows:

1 to 100 units	–	$0.20 per unit
101 to 200 units	–	$0.30 per unit
201 to 299 units	–	$0.40 per unit

with only the additional units qualifying for the higher rates. Rejected units do not qualify for payment.

During a particular day the employee produced 210 units of which 17 were rejected as faulty.

What did the employee earn for their day's work?

A $47.90
B $54.00
C $57.90
D $63.00   **(2 marks)**

7.6 Employee A is a carpenter and normally works 36 hours per week. The standard rate of pay is $3.60 per hour. A premium of 50% of the basic hourly rate is paid for all overtime hours worked. During the last week of October, Employee A worked for 42 hours. The overtime hours worked were for the following reasons:

Machine breakdown:	4 hours
To complete a special job at the request of a customer:	2 hours

How much of Employee A's earnings for the last week of October would have been treated as direct wages?

A $162.00
B $129.60
C $140.40
D $151.20 **(2 marks)**

7.7 Which of the following statements is/are true about group bonus schemes?

(i) Group bonus schemes are appropriate when increased output depends on a number of people all making extra effort
(ii) With a group bonus scheme, it is easier to award each individual's performance
(iii) Non-production employees can be rewarded as part of a group incentive scheme

A (i) only
B (i) and (ii) only
C (i) and (iii) only
D (ii) and (iii) only **(2 marks)**

7.8 X Co has recorded the following wages costs for direct production workers for November.

	$
Basic pay	70,800
Overtime premium	2,000
Holiday pay	500
Gross wages incurred	73,300

The overtime was not worked for any specific job.

The accounting entries for these wages costs would be:

		Debit $	Credit $
A	Work in progress account	72,800	
	Overhead control account	500	
	Wages control account		73,300
B	Work in progress account	70,800	
	Overhead control account	2,500	
	Wages control account		73,300
C	Wages control account	73,300	
	Work in progress account		70,800
	Overhead control account		2,500
D	Wages control account	73,300	
	Work in progress account		72,800
	Overhead control account		500

(2 marks)

7.9 A company had 30 direct production employees at the beginning of last year and 20 direct production employees at the end of the year. During the year, a total of 15 direct production employees had left the company to work for a local competitor. The labour turnover rate for last year was:

    A   16.7%
    B   20.0%
    C   25.0%
    D   60.0%   **(2 marks)**

7.10 Jane works as a member of a three-person team in the assembly department of a factory. The team is rewarded by a group bonus scheme whereby the team leader receives 40 per cent of any bonus earned by the team, and the remaining bonus is shared evenly between Jane and the other team member. Details of output for one day are given below.

Hours worked by team	8 hours
Team production achieved	80 units
Standard time allowed to produce one unit	9 minutes
Group bonus payable at $6 per hour	70% of time saved

The bonus element of Jane's pay for this particular day will be

    A $5.04
    B $7.20
    C $10.08
    D $16.80   **(2 marks)**

7.11 In a typical cost ledger, the double entry for indirect labour cost incurred is:

A	DR	Wages control	CR	Overhead control
B	DR	Admin overhead control	CR	Wages control
C	DR	Overhead control	CR	Wages control
D	DR	Wages control	CR	Admin overhead control

       (2 marks)

       (Total = 22 marks)

Do you know? – Absorption costing and marginal costing

Check that you can fill in the blanks in the statements below before you attempt any questions. If in doubt, you should go back to your BPP Interactive Text and revise first.

- Costs incurred during production or while providing a service that cannot be traced directly and in full to the product or service are known as ...., and the four main types of .... are production, administration, ... and distribution.

- The three stages of calculating the costs of overheads to be charged to manufactured output are as follows: .... ; .... ; and ....

- The procedure whereby indirect costs (overheads) are spread fairly between cost centres is known as .... Service cost centres may be apportioned to production cost centres by the .... method or by the .... method of reapportionment.

- The three main types of overhead absorption rate are as follows.

  .... (calculated by dividing budgeted overhead by budgeted level of activity)

  .... (or blanket overhead absorption rate, which is used throughout a factory for all jobs and units of output irrespective of the department in which they were produced)

  .... (a fairer rate which is representative of the costs of the resources put into making products)

- Under and over absorption of overhead occurs when actual overhead incurred is different to absorbed overhead. ....-absorbed overhead occurs when actual overhead is less than absorbed overhead, and therefore too .... overhead has been charged to production. ....-absorbed overhead occurs when actual overhead is greater than absorbed overhead, and therefore too .... overhead has been charged to production. Under or over absorption of overheads occurs because the predetermined overhead absorption rates are based on forecasts (estimates).

- Marginal cost is the .... cost of one unit of product or service. .... is the difference between the sales value and the marginal cost of one unit of product or service.

- In marginal costing, fixed production costs are treated as .... costs and are written off as they are incurred. In absorption costing fixed production costs are .... the cost of units and are carried forward in inventory to be charged against the sales revenue for the next period. Inventory values using absorption costing are therefore .... than those calculated using marginal costing.

- Marginal costing and absorption costing will report different profit figures if there is any change in the volume of inventory during the period. If closing inventory is greater than opening inventory, absorption costing will report a .... profit than marginal costing. If opening inventory is greater than closing inventory (ie inventory levels ....), then absorption costing will report a .... profit than marginal costing.

- *Possible pitfalls*

  Write down the mistakes you know you should avoid.

31

Did you know? – Absorption costing and marginal costing

Could you fill in the blanks? The answers are in bold. Use this page for revision purposes as you approach the exam.

- Costs incurred during production or while providing a service that cannot be traced directly and in full to the product or service are known as **overheads**, and the four main types of **overhead** are production, administration, **selling** and distribution.

- The three stages of calculating the costs of overheads to be charged to manufactured output are as follows: **allocation; apportionment;** and **absorption.**

- The procedure whereby indirect costs (overheads) are spread fairly between cost centres is known as **apportionment**. Service cost centres may be apportioned to production cost centres by the **direct** method or by the **step down** method of reapportionment.

- The three main types of overhead absorption rate are as follows.

  Predetermined overhead absorption rate (calculated by dividing budgeted overhead by budgeted level of activity)

  Single factory-wide absorption rate (or blanket overhead absorption rate, which is used throughout a factory for all jobs and units of output irrespective of the department in which they were produced)

  Separate departmental overhead absorption rate (a fairer rate which is representative of the costs of the resources put into making products)

- Under and over absorption of overhead occurs when actual overhead incurred is different to absorbed overhead. **Over**-absorbed overhead occurs when actual overhead is less than absorbed overhead, and therefore too **much** overhead has been charged to production. **Under**-absorbed overhead occurs when actual overhead is greater than absorbed overhead, and therefore too **little** overhead has been charged to production. Under or overabsorption of overheads occurs because the predetermined overhead absorption rates are based on forecasts (estimates).

- Marginal cost is the **variable** cost of one unit of product or service. **Contribution** is the difference between the sales value and the marginal cost of one unit of product or service.

- In marginal costing, fixed production costs are treated as **period** costs and are written off as they are incurred. In absorption costing fixed production costs are **absorbed into** the cost of units and are carried forward in inventory to be charged against the sales revenue for the next period. Inventory values using absorption costing are therefore **greater** than those calculated using marginal costing.

- Marginal costing and absorption costing will report different profit figures if there is any change in the volume of inventory during the period. If closing inventory is greater than opening inventory, absorption costing will report a **higher** profit than marginal costing. If opening inventory is greater than closing inventory (ie inventory levels **decrease**), then absorption costing will report a **lower** profit than marginal costing.

- *Possible pitfalls*

  Including an element of fixed overheads in the inventory valuation in marginal costing statements
  Selecting inappropriate bases when calculating overhead absorption rates
  Confusing under recovery and over recovery of overheads

8 Accounting for overheads   48 mins

8.1   The following extract of information is available concerning the four cost centres of EG Limited.

	Production cost centres			Service cost centre
	Machinery	Finishing	Packing	Canteen
Number of direct employees	7	6	2	–
Number of indirect employees	3	2	1	4
Overhead allocated and apportioned	$28,500	$18,300	$8,960	$8,400

The overhead cost of the canteen is to be re-apportioned to the production cost centres on the basis of the number of employees in each production cost centre. After the re-apportionment, the total overhead cost of the packing department, to the nearest $, will be

A $1,200
B $9,968
C $10,080
D $10,160   (2 marks)

The following information relates to questions 8.2 and 8.3

Budgeted information relating to two departments in a company for the next period is as follows.

Department	Production overhead $	Direct material cost $	Direct labour cost $	Direct labour hours	Machine hours
1	27,000	67,500	13,500	2,700	45,000
2	18,000	36,000	100,000	25,000	300

Individual direct labour employees within each department earn differing rates of pay, according to their skills, grade and experience.

8.2   What is the most appropriate production overhead absorption rate for department 1?

A   40% of direct material cost
B   200% of direct labour cost
C $10 per direct labour hour
D $0.60 per machine hour   (2 marks)

8.3   What is the most appropriate production overhead absorption rate for department 2?

A   50% of direct material cost
B   18% of direct labour cost
C $0.72 per direct labour hour
D $60 per machine hour   (2 marks)

8.4   Which of the following statements about predetermined overhead absorption rates are true?

(i)   Using a predetermined absorption rate avoids fluctuations in unit costs caused by abnormally high or low overhead expenditure or activity levels
(ii)   Using a predetermined absorption rate offers the administrative convenience of being able to record full production costs sooner
(iii) Using a predetermined absorption rate avoids problems of under/over absorption of overheads because a constant overhead rate is available.

A   (i) and (ii) only
B   (i) and (iii) only
C   (ii) and (iii) only
D   All of them   (2 marks)

8.5 Over-absorbed overheads occur when

A   Absorbed overheads exceed actual overheads
B   Absorbed overheads exceed budgeted overheads
C   Actual overheads exceed absorbed overheads
D   Actual overheads exceed budgeted overheads   (2 marks)

The following information relates to questions 8.6 and 8.7

A company has the following actual and budgeted data for year 4.

	Budget	Actual
Production	8,000 units	9,000 units
Variable production overhead per unit	$3	$3
Fixed production overheads	$360,000	$432,000
Sales	6,000 units	8,000 units

Overheads are absorbed using a rate per unit, based on budgeted output and expenditure.

8.6 The fixed production overhead absorbed during year 4 was:

A $384,000
B $405,000
C $432,000
D $459,000   (2 marks)

8.7 Fixed production overhead was:

A   under absorbed by $27,000
B   under absorbed by $72,000
C   under absorbed by $75,000
D   over absorbed by $27,000   (2 marks)

8.8 Which of the following would be the most appropriate basis for apportioning machinery insurance costs to cost centres within a factory?

A   The number of machines in each cost centre
B   The floor area occupied by the machinery in each cost centre
C   The value of the machinery in each cost centre
D   The operating hours of the machinery in each cost centre   (2 marks)

8.9 Factory overheads can be absorbed by which of the following methods?

(i)   Direct labour hours
(ii)   Machine hours
(iii)   As a percentage of prime cost
(iv) $x per unit

A   (i), (ii), (iii) and (iv)
B   (i) and (ii) only
C   (i), (ii) and (iii) only
D   (ii), (iii) and (iv) only   (2 marks)

8.10 The production overhead control account for R Limited at the end of the period looks like this.

PRODUCTION OVERHEAD CONTROL ACCOUNT

	$		$
Stores control	22,800	Work in progress	404,800
Wages control	180,400	Profit and loss	8,400
Expense creditors	210,000		
	413,200		413,200

Which of the following statements are correct?

(i) Indirect material issued from inventory was $22,800
(ii) Overhead absorbed during the period was $210,000
(iii) Overhead for the period was over absorbed by $8,400
(iv) Indirect wages costs incurred were $180,400

A (i), (ii) and (iii)
B (i), (iii) and (iv)
C (i) and (iv)
D All of them   **(2 marks)**

8.11 Which of the following is correct when considering the allocation, apportionment and reapportionment of overheads in an absorption costing situation?

A Only production related costs should be considered
B Allocation is the situation where part of an overhead is assigned to a cost centre
C Costs may only be reapportioned from production centres to service centres
D Any overheads assigned to a single department should be ignored   **(2 marks)**

8.12 A company has over-absorbed fixed production overheads for the period by $6,000. The fixed production overhead absorption rate was $8 per unit and is based on the normal level of activity of 5,000 units. Actual production was 4,500 units.

What was the actual fixed production overheads incurred for the period?

A $30,000
B $36,000
C $40,000
D $42,000   **(2 marks)**

8.13 A company manufacturers two products, X and Y, in a factory divided into two production cost centres, Primary and Finishing. The following budgeted data are available:

Cost centre	Primary	Finishing
Allocated and apportioned fixed overhead costs	$96,000	$82,500
Direct labour minutes per unit:		
– product X	36	25
– product Y	48	35

Budgeted production is 6,000 units of product X and 7,500 units of product Y. Fixed overhead costs are to be absorbed on a direct labour hour basis.

What is the budgeted fixed overhead cost per unit for product Y?

A $11
B $12
C $14
D $15   **(2 marks)**

8.14 A company uses an overhead absorption rate of $3.50 per machine our, based on 32,000 budgeted machine hours for the period. During the same period the actual total overhead expenditure amounted to $108,875 and 30,000 machine hours were recorded on actual production.

By how much was the total overhead under or over absorbed for the period?

A   Under absorbed by $3,875
B   Under absorbed by $7,000
C   Over absorbed by $3,875
D   Over absorbed by $7,000   **(2 marks)**

8.15 A factory consists of two production cost centres (P and Q) and two service cost centres (X and Y). The total allocated and apportioned overhead for each is as follows:

P	Q	X	Y
$95,000	$82,000	$46,000	$30,000

It has been estimated that each service cost centre does work for the other cost centres in the following proportions:

	P	Q	X	Y
Percentage of service cost centre X to	40	40	–	20
Percentage of service cost centre Y to	30	60	10	–

After the reapportionment of service cost centre costs has been carried out using a method that fully recognises the reciprocal service arrangements in the factory, what is the total overhead for production cost centre P?

A $122,400
B $124,716
C $126,000
D $127,000   **(2 marks)**

8.16 The following data is available for a paint department for the latest period.

Budgeted production overhead	$150,000
Actual production overhead	$150,000
Budgeted machine hours	60,000
Actual machine hours	55,000

Which of the following statements is correct?

A   There was no under or over absorption of overhead
B   Overhead was $13,636 over absorbed
C   Overhead was $12,500 over absorbed
D   Overhead was $12,500 under absorbed   **(2 marks)**

8.17

Actual overheads	$496,980
Actual machine hours	16,566
Budgeted overheads	$475,200

Based on the data above, and assuming that the budgeted overhead absorption rate was $32 per hour, the number of machine hours (to the nearest hour) budgeted to be worked were ⬚ hours.

A   14,850
B   15,531
C   16,566
D   33,132   **(2 marks)**

8.18

Budgeted overheads	$690,480
Budgeted machine hours	15,344
Actual machine hours	14,128
Actual overheads	$679,550

Based on the data above, the machine hour absorption rate is (to the nearest $)

$ ☐ per machine hour.

A   44
B   45
C   48
D   49   **(2 marks)**

8.19   A company absorbs overheads on machine hours. In a period, actual machine hours were 22,435, actual overheads were $496,500 and there was over absorption of $64,375.

The budgeted overhead absorption rate was $ ☐ per machine hour (to the nearest $).

A   19
B   22
C   25
D   27   **(2 marks)**

8.20   A company absorbs fixed production overheads in one of its departments on the basis of machine hours. There were 100,000 budgeted machine hours for the forthcoming period. The fixed production overhead absorption rate was $2.50 per machine hour.

During the period, the following actual results were recorded:

Standard machine hours	110,000
Fixed production overheads	$300,000

Fixed production overhead was ☐ absorbed by $ ☐

A   Over absorbed by $25,000
B   Under absorbed by $50,000
C   Over absorbed by $50,000
D   Under absorbed by $25,000   **(2 marks)**

(Total = 40 marks)

9 Absorption costing and marginal costing   43 mins

9.1   The following data is available for period 9.

Opening inventory   10,000 units
Closing inventory   8,000 units
Absorption costing profit $280,000

The profit for period 9 using marginal costing would be:

A $278,000
B $280,000
C $282,000
D   Impossible to calculate without more information   **(2 marks)**

9.2   The overhead absorption rate for product T is $4 per machine hour. Each unit of T requires 3 machine hours. Inventories of product T last period were:

	Units
Opening inventory	2,400
Closing inventory	2,700

Compared with the marginal costing profit for the period, the absorption costing profit for product T will be:

A $1,200 higher
B $3,600 higher
C $1,200 lower
D $3,600 lower   **(2 marks)**

9.3   In a period where opening inventories were 15,000 units and closing inventories were 20,000 units, a firm had a profit of $130,000 using absorption costing. If the fixed overhead absorption rate was $8 per unit, the profit using marginal costing would be:

A $90,000
B $130,000
C $170,000
D   Impossible to calculate without more information   **(2 marks)**

The following information relates to questions 9.4 and 9.5

Cost and selling price details for product Z are as follows.

	$ per unit
Direct materials	6.00
Direct labour	7.50
Variable overhead	2.50
Fixed overhead absorption rate	5.00
	21.00
Profit	9.00
Selling price	30.00

Budgeted production for the month was 5,000 units although the company managed to produce 5,800 units, selling 5,200 of them and incurring fixed overhead costs of $27,400.

9.4   The marginal costing profit for the month is:

A $45,400
B $46,800
C $53,800
D $72,800   **(2 marks)**

9.5   The absorption costing profit for the month is:

    A $45,200   C $46,800
    B $45,400   D $48,400   **(2 marks)**

9.6   In a period, a company had opening inventory of 31,000 units and closing inventory of 34,000 units. Profits based on marginal costing were $850,500 and on absorption costing were $955,500.

    If the budgeted total fixed costs for the company was $1,837,500, what was the budgeted level of activity in units?

    A   32,500   C   65,000
    B   52,500   D   105,000   **(2 marks)**

9.7   A company had opening inventory of 48,500 units and closing inventory of 45,500 units. Profits based on marginal costing were $315,250 and on absorption costing were $288,250. What is the fixed overhead absorption rate per unit?

    A $5.94   C $6.50
    B $6.34   D $9.00   **(2 marks)**

9.8   Which of the following are acceptable bases for absorbing production overheads?

    (i)   Direct labour hours
    (ii)   Machine hours
    (iii)   As a percentage of the prime cost
    (iv)   Per unit

    A   Method (i) and (ii) only
    B   Method (iii) and (iv) only
    C   Method (i), (ii), (iii) and (iv)
    D   Method (i), (ii) or (iii) only   **(2 marks)**

9.9   Absorption costing is concerned with which of the following?

    A   Direct materials
    B   Direct labour
    C   Fixed costs
    D   Variable and fixed costs   **(2 marks)**

9.10   A company has established a marginal costing profit of $72,300. Opening inventory was 300 units and closing inventory is 750 units. The fixed production overhead absorption rate has been calculated as $5/unit.

    What was the profit under absorption costing?

    A $67,050
    B $70,050
    C $74,550
    D $77,550   **(2 marks)**

9.11   A company produces and sells a single product whose variable cost is $6 per unit.

    Fixed costs have been absorbed over the normal level of activity of 200,000 units and have been calculated as $2 per unit.

    The current selling price is $10 per unit.

    How much profit is made under marginal costing if the company sells 250,000 units?

    A $500,000
    B $600,000
    C $900,000
    D $1,000,000   **(2 marks)**

9.12 A company wishes to make a profit of $150,000. It has fixed costs of $75,000 with a C/S ratio of 0.75 and a selling price of $10 per unit.

How many units would the company need to sell in order to achieve the required level of profit?

A   10,000 units
B   15,000 units
C   22,500 units
D   30,000 units   **(2 marks)**

9.13 A company which uses marginal costing has a profit of $37,500 for a period. Opening inventory was 100 units and closing inventory was 350 units.

The fixed production overhead absorption rate is $4 per unit.

What is the profit under absorption costing?

A $35,700
B $35,500
C $38,500
D $39,300   **(2 marks)**

9.14 A company manufactures and sells a single product. For this month the budgeted fixed production overheads are $48,000, budgeted production is 12,000 units and budgeted sales are 11,720 units.

The company currently uses absorption costing.

If the company used marginal costing principles instead of absorption costing for this month, what would be the effect on the budgeted profit?

A $1,120 higher
B $1,120 lower
C $3,920 higher
D $3,920 lower   **(2 marks)**

9.15 A company operates a standard marginal costing system. Last month its actual fixed overhead expenditure was 10% above budget resulting in a fixed overhead expenditure variance of $36,000.

What was the actual expenditure on fixed overheads last month?

A $324,000
B $360,000
C $396,000
D $400,000   **(2 marks)**

9.16 Last month, when a company had an opening inventory of 16,500 units and a closing inventory of 18,000 units, the profit using absorption costing was $40,000. The fixed production overhead rate was $10 per unit.

What would the profit for last month have been using marginal costing?

A $15,000
B $25,000
C $55,000
D $65,000   **(2 marks)**

9.17 Last month a manufacturing company's profit was $2,000, calculated using absorption costing principles. If marginal costing principles has been used, a loss of $3,000 would have occurred. The company's fixed production cost is $2 per unit. Sales last month were 10,000 units.

What was last month's production (in units)?

A   7,500   B   9,500   C   10,500   D   12,500

                                                                                (2 marks)

9.18 HMF Co produces a single product. The budgeted fixed production overheads for the period are $500,000. The budgeted output for the period is 2,500 units. Opening inventory at the start of the period consisted of 900 units and closing inventory at the end of the period consisted of 300 units. If absorption costing principles were applied, the profit for the period compared to the marginal costing profit would be:

A $125,000 higher
B $125,000 lower
C $120,000 higher
D $120,000 lower

(2 marks)

(Total = 36 marks)

Do you know? – Process, job, batch, service and alternative costing

Check that you can fill in the blanks in the statements below before you attempt any questions. If in doubt, you should go back to your BPP Interactive Text and revise first.

- Process costing is a costing method used where it is not possible to identify separate units of production usually because of the continuous nature of the production processes involved.

- .... loss is the loss expected during a process and it is not given a cost. If it has a scrap value then it is valued at this amount.

- .... loss is the extra loss resulting when actual loss is greater than the loss anticipated. It is given a cost.

- Loss may have a scrap value. Revenue from normal scrap is treated as a reduction in costs.

- When there is closing work in progress at the end of a period, it is necessary to calculate the .... of production in order to determine the cost of a completed unit.

- The costs of labour and overhead are sometimes referred to as .... costs.

- .... products are two or more products separated in a process, each of which has a significant value compared to the other.

- A .... is an incidental product from a process which has an insignificant value compared to the main product.

- The point at which joint and by-products become separately identifiable is known as the .... or the .... point

- Job costing is the costing method used where each cost unit is separately identifiable. Costs for each job are collected on a .... or .... Overhead is absorbed into the cost of jobs using the .... rate.

- Batch costing is similar to job costing in that each batch of similar articles is separately identifiable. The cost per unit manufactured in a batch is calculated by dividing the .... by the .... in the batch.

- Service costing is used by companies operating in a service industry or by companies wishing to establish the cost of services carried out by some of their departments.

- Characteristics of services
  - ....
  - ....
  - ....
  - ....

- If a service is a function of two activity variables, a .... cost unit might be appropriate.

- A difficulty with service costing is the selection of an appropriate cost unit. The cost per unit is calculated by dividing the .... for the period by the .... in the period.

- Activity based costing involves the identification of factors, called cost .... which cause costs

- .... costing tracks and accumulates costs and revenues attributable to each product over the entire ....

- *Possible pitfalls*

  Write down the mistakes you know you should avoid.

Did you know? – Process, job, batch, service and alternative costing

Could you fill in the blanks? The answers are in bold. Use this page for revision purposes as you approach the exam.

- Process costing is a costing method used where it is not possible to identify separate units of production usually because of the continuous nature of the production processes involved.

- **Normal** loss is the loss expected during a process and it is not given a cost. If it has a scrap value then it is valued at this amount.

- **Abnormal** loss is the extra loss resulting when actual loss is greater than the loss anticipated. It is given a cost.

- Loss may have a scrap value. Revenue from normal scrap is treated as a reduction in costs.

- When there is closing work in progress at the end of a period, it is necessary to calculate the **equivalent units** of production in order to determine the cost of a completed unit.

- The costs of labour and overhead are sometimes referred to as **conversion** costs.

- **Joint** products are two or more products separated in a process, each of which has a significant value compared to the other.

- A **by-product** is an incidental product from a process which has an insignificant value compared to the main product.

- The point at which joint and by-products become separately identifiable is known as the **point of separation** or the **split-off** point.

- Job costing is the costing method used where each cost unit is separately identifiable. Costs for each job are collected on a **job cost sheet** or **job card**. Overhead is absorbed into the cost of jobs using the **predetermined overhead absorption** rate.

- Batch costing is similar to job costing in that each batch of similar articles is separately identifiable. The cost per unit manufactured in a batch is calculated by dividing the **total batch cost** by the **number of units** in the batch.

- Service costing is used by companies operating in a service industry or by companies wishing to establish the cost of services carried out by some of their departments.

- Characteristics of services**: Intangibility, Simultaneity, Perishability, Heterogeneity**

- If a service is a function of two activity variables, a **composite** cost unit might be appropriate.

- A difficulty with service costing is the selection of an appropriate cost unit. The cost per unit is calculated by dividing the **total costs** for the period by the **number of service units** in the period.

- Activity based costing involves the identification of factors, called cost **drivers** which cause costs

- **Life cycle** costing tracks and accumulates costs and revenues attributable to each product over the entire **product life cycle**

- *Possible pitfalls*

  Forgetting that units arising from abnormal loss are included as equivalent units, whereas those arising from normal loss are not

  Not using the suggested four-step approach when answering process costing questions

10 Job, batch and service costing   36 mins

10.1   Which of the following costing methods is most likely to be used by a company involved in the manufacture of liquid soap?

   A   Batch costing
   B   Service costing
   C   Job costing
   D   Process costing   **(2 marks)**

10.2   A company calculates the prices of jobs by adding overheads to the prime cost and adding 30% to total costs as a mark up. Job number Y256 was sold for $1,690 and incurred overheads of $694. What was the prime cost of the job?

   A $489
   B $606
   C $996
   D $1,300   **(2 marks)**

10.3   A company operates a job costing system.

The estimated costs for job 173 are as follows.

Direct materials   5 metres @ $20 per metre
Direct labour   14 hours @ $8 per hour

Variable production overheads are recovered at the rate of $3 per direct labour hour.

Fixed production overheads for the year are budgeted to be $200,000 and are to be recovered on the basis of the total of 40,000 direct labour hours for the year.

Other overheads, in relation to selling, distribution and administration, are recovered at the rate of $80 per job.

The total cost of job 173 is

   A $404   B $300   C $254   D $324
                                                                             (2 marks)

The following information relates to questions 10.4 and 10.5

A firm makes special assemblies to customers' orders and uses job costing.

The data for a period are:

	Job number AA10 $	Job number BB15 $	Job number CC20 $
Opening WIP	26,800	42,790	0
Material added in period	17,275	0	18,500
Labour for period	14,500	3,500	24,600

The budgeted overheads for the period were $126,000.

10.4   What overhead should be added to job number CC20 for the period?

   A $65,157
   B $69,290
   C $72,761
   D $126,000   **(2 marks)**

10.5 What was the approximate value of closing work-in-progress at the end of the period?

    A $58,575
    B $101,675
    C $217,323
    D $227,675   **(2 marks)**

10.6 The following items may be used in costing batches.

    1   Actual material cost
    2   Actual manufacturing overheads
    3   Absorbed manufacturing overheads
    4   Actual labour cost

Which of the above are contained in a typical batch cost?

    A   1, 2 and 4 only
    B   1 and 4 only
    C   1, 3 and 4 only
    D   1, 2, 3 and 4   **(2 marks)**

10.7 What would be the most appropriate cost unit for a cake manufacturer?

Cost per:

    A   Cake
    B   Batch
    C   Kg
    D   Piece of cake   **(2 marks)**

10.8 Which of the following would be appropriate cost units for a passenger coach company?

    (i)   Vehicle cost per passenger-kilometre
    (ii)   Fuel cost for each vehicle per kilometre
    (iii)   Fixed cost per kilometre

    A (i) only   B (i) and (ii) only   C (i) and (iii) only   D (ii) and (iii) only

        (2 marks)

10.9 The following information is available for a hotel company for the latest thirty day period.

Number of rooms available per night   40
Percentage occupancy achieved   65%
Room servicing cost incurred $3,900

The room servicing cost per occupied room-night last period, to the nearest penny, was:

    A $3.25   B $5.00   C $97.50   D $150.00

        (2 marks)

10.10 Annie is to set up a small hairdressing business at home. She anticipates working a 35-hour week and taking four weeks' holiday per year. Her expenses for materials and overheads are expected to be $3,000 per year, and she has set herself a target profit of $18,000 for the first year.

Assuming that only 90% of her working time will be chargeable to clients, what price should she charge for a 'colour and cut' which would take 3 hours?

    A $13.89
    B $35.71
    C $37.50
    D $41.67   **(2 marks)**

10.11 Which of the following is **not** a characteristic of service costing?

    A   High levels of direct costs as a proportion of total costs
    B   Intangibility of output
    C   Use of composite cost units
    D   Can be used for internal services as well as external services   **(2 marks)**

10.12 Which of the following are likely to use service costing?

    (i)   A college
    (ii)   A hotel
    (iii)   A plumber

    A   (i), (ii) and (iii)
    B   (i) and (ii)
    C   (ii) only
    D   (ii) and (iii) only   **(2 marks)**

10.13 Which of the following would be considered a service industry?

    (i)   An airline company
    (ii)   A railway company
    (iii)   A firm of accountants

    A   (i) and (ii) only
    B   (i) and (iii) only
    C   (i), (ii) and (iii)
    D   (ii) and (iii) only   **(2 marks)**

10.14 The following information relates to a management consultancy organisation:

	$
Salary cost per hour for senior consultants	40
Salary cost per hour for junior consultants	25
Overhead absorption rate per hour applied to all hours	20

The organisation adds 40% to total cost to arrive at the final fee to be charged to a client.

Assignment number 789 took 54 hours of a senior consultant's time and 110 hours of junior consultants' time.

What is the final fee to be charged for Assignment 789?

    A $6,874   C $11,466
    B $10,696   D $12,642   **(2 marks)**

10.15 A company operates a job costing system. Job number 1012 requires $45 of direct materials and $30 of direct labour. Direct labour is paid at the rate of $7.50 per hour. Production overheads are absorbed at a rate of $12.50 per direct labour hour and non-production overheads are absorbed at a rate of 60% of prime cost.

What is the total cost of job number 1012?

    A $170
    B $195
    C $200
    D $240   **(2 marks)**

(Total = 30 marks)

11 Process costing   36 mins

11.1 A chemical process has a normal wastage of 10% of input. In a period, 2,500 kgs of material were input and there was an abnormal loss of 75 kgs.

What quantity of good production was achieved?

A   2,175 kgs   B   2,250 kgs   C   2,325 kgs   D   2,425 kgs

(2 marks)

The following information relates to questions 11.2 and 11.3

A company manufactures Chemical X, in a single process. At the start of the month there was no work-in-progress. During the month 300 litres of raw material were input into the process at a total cost of $6,000. Conversion costs during the month amounted to $4,500. At the end of the month 250 litres of Chemical X were transferred to finished goods inventory. The remaining work-in-progress was 100% complete with respect to materials and 50% complete with respect to conversion costs. There were no losses in the process.

11.2 The equivalent units for closing work-in-progress at the end of the month would have been:

	Material	Conversion costs
A	25 litres	25 litres
B	25 litres	50 litres
C	50 litres	25 litres
D	50 litres	50 litres

(2 marks)

11.3 If there had been a normal process loss of 10% of input during the month the value of this loss would have been:

A   Nil
B $450
C $600
D $1,050

(2 marks)

11.4 In a particular process, the input for the period was 2,000 units. There were no inventories at the beginning or end of the process. Normal loss is 5 per cent of input. In which of the following circumstances is there an abnormal gain?

(i)   Actual output = 1,800 units
(ii)   Actual output = 1,950 units
(iii) Actual output = 2,000 units

A   (i) only
B   (ii) only
C   (i) and (ii) only
D   (ii) and (iii) only

(2 marks)

11.5 In a process account, abnormal losses are valued:

A   At their scrap value
B   The same as good production
C   At the cost of raw materials
D   The same as normal losses

(2 marks)

11.6 A company needs to produce 340 litres of Chemical X. There is a normal loss of 10% of the material input into the process. During a given month the company did produce 340 litres of good production, although there was an abnormal loss of 5% of the material input into the process.

How many litres of material were input into the process during the month?

A   357 litres   B   374 litres   C   391 litres   D   400 litres

(2 marks)

The following information relates to questions 11.7 and 11.8

A company produces a certain food item in a manufacturing process. On 1 November, there was no opening inventory of work in process. During November, 500 units of material were input to the process, with a cost of $9,000. Direct labour costs in November were $3,840. Production overhead is absorbed at the rate of 200% of direct labour costs. Closing inventory on 30 November consisted of 100 units which were 100% complete as to materials and 80% complete as to labour and overhead. There was no loss in process.

11.7 The full production cost of completed units during November was

A $10,400
B $16,416
C $16,800
D $20,520

(2 marks)

11.8 The value of the closing work in progress on 30 November is

A $2,440
B $3,720
C $4,104
D $20,520

(2 marks)

The following information relates to questions 11.9 and 11.10

A company makes a product in two processes. The following data is available for the latest period, for process 1.

Opening work in progress of 200 units was valued as follows.

Material	$2,400
Labour	$1,200
Overhead	$400

No losses occur in the process.

Units added and costs incurred during the period:

Material	$6,000 (500 units)
Labour	$3,350
Overhead	$1,490

Closing work in progress of 100 units had reached the following degrees of completion:

Material	100%
Labour	50%
Overhead	30%

The company uses the weighted average method of inventory valuation.

11.9 How many equivalent units are used when calculating the cost per unit in relation to overhead?

A   500   B   600   C   630   D   700

(2 marks)

11.10 The value of the units transferred to process 2 was

A $7,200   B $13,200   C $14,840   D $15,400

(2 marks)

11.11 A company uses process costing to establish the cost per unit of its output.

The following information was available for the last month:

Input units	10,000
Output units	9,850
Opening inventory	300 units, 100% complete for materials and 70% complete for conversion costs
Closing inventory	450 units, 100% complete for materials and 30% complete for conversion costs

The company uses the weighted average method of valuing inventory.

What were the equivalent units for conversion costs?

A   9,505 units
B   9,715 units
C   9,775 units
D   9,985 units

(2 marks)

11.12 A company uses process costing to value its output. The following was recorded for the period;

Input materials	2,000 units at $4.50 per unit
Conversion costs	13,340
Normal loss	5% of input valued at $3 per unit
Actual loss	150 units

There were no opening or closing inventories.

What was the valuation of one unit of output to one decimal place?

A $11.8
B $11.6
C $11.2
D $11.0

(2 marks)

11.13 A company operates a continuous process into which 3,000 units of material costing $9,000 was input in a period. Conversion costs for this period were $11,970 and losses, which have a scrap value of $1.50, are expected at a rate of 10% of input. There were no opening or closing inventories and output for the period was 2,900 units.

What was the output valuation?

A $20,271
B $20,520
C $20,970
D $22,040

(2 marks)

11.14 The following information relates to a company's polishing process for the previous period.

Output to finished goods	5,408 units valued at $29,744
Normal loss	276 units
Actual loss	112 units

All losses have a scrap value of $2.50 per unit and there was no opening or closing work in progress.

The value of the input during the period was:

A $28,842
B $29,532
C $29,744
D $30,434

(2 marks)

11.15 Which of the following statements about process losses are correct?

(i)   Units of normal loss should be valued at full cost per unit.
(ii)   Units of abnormal loss should be valued at their scrap value.

A   (i) only
B   (ii) only
C   Both of them
D   Neither of them   **(2 marks)**

(Total = 30 marks)

12   Process costing, joint and by-products   17 mins

The following data relates to questions 12.1 and 12.2

A company manufactures two joint products, P and R, in a common process. Data for June are as follows.

	$
Opening inventory	1,000
Direct materials added	10,000
Conversion costs	12,000
Closing inventory	3,000

	Production Units	Sales Units	Sales price $ per unit
P	4,000	5,000	5
R	6,000	5,000	10

12.1 If costs are apportioned between joint products on a sales value basis, what was the cost per unit of product R in June?

A $1.25
B $2.22
C $2.50
D $2.75   **(2 marks)**

12.2 If costs are apportioned between joint products on a physical unit basis, what was the total cost of product P production in June?

A $8,000
B $8,800
C $10,000
D $12,000   **(2 marks)**

12.3 Which of the following statements is/are correct?

(i)   A by-product is a product produced at the same time as other products which has a relatively low volume compared with the other products.
(ii)   Since a by-product is a saleable item it should be separately costed in the process account, and should absorb some of the process costs.
(iii) Costs incurred prior to the point of separation are known as common or joint costs.

A   (i) and (ii)
B   (i) and (iii)
C   (ii) and (iii)
D   (iii) only   **(2 marks)**

12.4   A company manufactures two joint products and one by-product in a single process. Data for November are as follows.

	$
Raw material input	216,000
Conversion costs	72,000

There were no inventories at the beginning or end of the period.

	Output Units	Sales price $ per unit
Joint product E	21,000	15
Joint product Q	18,000	10
By-product X	2,000	2

By-product sales revenue is credited to the process account. Joint costs are apportioned on a sales value basis. What were the full production costs of product Q in November (to the nearest $)?

A $102,445
B $103,273
C $104,727
D $180,727   **(2 marks)**

12.5   A company manufactures three joint products and one by-product from a single process.

Data for May are as follows.

Opening and closing inventories	Nil
Raw materials input	$180,000
Conversion costs	$50,000

Output

		Units	Sales price $ per unit
Joint product	L	3,000	32
	M	2,000	42
	N	4,000	38
By-product R		1,000	2

By-product sales revenue is credited to the sales account. Joint costs are apportioned on a sales value basis.

What were the full production costs of product M in May (to the nearest $)?

A $57,687
B $57,844
C $58,193
D $66,506   **(2 marks)**

12.6 Two products G and H are created from a joint process. G can be sold immediately after split-off. H requires further processing before it is in a saleable condition. There are no opening inventories and no work in progress. The following data are available for last period:

	$
Total joint production costs	384,000
Further processing costs (product H)	159,600

Product	Selling price per unit	Sales Units	Production Units
G	$0.84	400,000	412,000
H	$1.82	200,000	228,000

Using the physical unit method for apportioning joint production costs, what was the cost value of the closing inventory of product H for last period?

A $36,400   B $37,520   C $40,264   D $45,181

(2 marks)

12.7 Two products (W and X) are created from a joint process. Both products can be sold immediately after split-off. There are no opening inventories or work in progress. The following information is available for last period:

Total joint production costs $776,160

Product	Production units	Sales units	Selling price per unit
W	12,000	10,000	$10
X	10,000	8,000	$12

Using the sales value method of apportioning joint production costs, what was the value of the closing inventory of product X for last period?

A $310,464   B $388,080   C $155,232   D $77,616

(2 marks)

(Total = 14 marks)

13 Alternative costing principles   14 mins

13.1 Which of the following statements is not correct?

A   Activity based costing is an alternative to traditional volume-based costing methods
B   Activity based costs provide an approximation of long-run variable unit costs
C   Activity based costing cannot be used to cost services
D   Activity based costing is a form of absorption costing   **(2 marks)**

13.2 A product is in the stage of its life cycle which is typified by falling prices but good profit margins due to high sales volumes. What stage is it in?

A   Growth
B   Maturity
C   Introduction
D   Decline   **(2 marks)**

13.3 Which of the following statements describes life cycle costing?

A   The profiling of cost over a product's production life
B   The profiling of cost over a product's development, production life and dismantling period
C   The profiling of cost and revenues over a product's development, production life and dismantling period
D   The profiling of cost and revenues over a product's production life   **(2 marks)**

13.4 In what stage of the product life cycle are initial costs of the investment in the product typically recovered?

A   Introduction
B   Decline
C   Growth
D   Maturity   **(2 marks)**

13.5 How is target cost calculated?

A   Desired selling price – actual profit margin
B   Market price – desired profit margin
C   Desired selling price – desired profit margin
D   Market price – standard profit margin   **(2 marks)**

13.6 Which stage of the product life cycle do the following characteristics refer to?

New competitors
Customer feedback received
New distribution outlets being found
Product quality improvements made

A   Growth
B   Decline
C   Maturity
D   Introduction   **(2 marks)**

(Total = 12 marks)

Do you know? – Forecasting and budgeting

Check that you can fill in the blanks in the statements below before you attempt any questions. If in doubt, you should go back to your BPP Interactive Text and revise first.

- A .... is a plan of what the organisation is aiming to achieve and what it has set as a target whereas a .... is an estimate of what is likely to occur in the future.

- The degree of correlation between two variables is measured by the ....

  r = +1 means that the variables are .... correlated .

  r = -1 means that the variables are .... correlated

  r = 0 means that the variables are ....

  The square of the correlation coefficient is called the .... of .... It measures the .... of the total variation in the value of one variable that can be explained by variations in the value of the other variable.

- Linear regression analysis is one method used for estimating a line of .... As with all forecasting techniques, the results from regression analysis will not be wholly reliable. There are a number of factors which affect the reliability of forecasts made using regression analysis. For example, it assumes that a .... exists between the two variables.

- A time series is a series of figures or values recorded over time. The time series analysis forecasting technique is usually used to ....

- There are four components of a time series: ...., ..., ... and ....

- One way of finding the trend is to use ....

- Management accountants will use spreadsheet software in activities such as budgeting, forecasting, reporting performance and variance analysis. Spreadsheet packages have the facility to perform ....-... calculations at great speed.

- The .... should be identified at the beginning of the budgetary process and the budget for this is prepared before all others.

- .... budgets include production budgets, marketing budgets, sales budgets, personnel budgets, purchasing budgets and research and development budgets.

- *Possible pitfalls*

  Write down the mistakes you know you should avoid.

Did you know? – Forecasting and budgeting

Could you fill in the blanks? The answers are in bold. Use this page for revision purposes as you approach the exam.

- A **budget** is a plan of what the organisation is aiming to achieve and what it has set as a target whereas a **forecast** is an estimate of what is likely to occur in the future.

- The degree of correlation between two variables is measured by the **correlation coefficient**.

  $r = +1$ means that the variables are **perfectly positively** correlated .

  $r = -1$ means that the variables are **perfectly negatively** correlated

  $r = 0$ means that the variables are **uncorrelated**

  The square of the correlation coefficient is called the **coefficient** of **determination** . It measures the **proportion** of the total variation in the value of one variable that can be explained by variations in the value of the other variable.

- Linear regression analysis is one method used for estimating a line of **best fit.** As with all forecasting techniques, the results from regression analysis will not be wholly reliable. There are a number of factors which affect the reliability of forecasts made using regression analysis. For example, it assumes that a **linear relationship** exists between the two variables.

- A time series is a series of figures or values recorded over time. The time series analysis forecasting technique is usually used to **forecast sales**

- There are four components of a time series: **trend, seasonal variations, cyclical variations and randon variations.**

- One way of finding the trend is to use **moving averages.**

- Management accountants will use spreadsheet software in activities such as budgeting, forecasting, reporting performance and variance analysis. Spreadsheet packages have the facility to perform **what-if** calculations at great speed.

- The **principal budget factor** should be identified at the beginning of the budgetary process and the budget for this is prepared before all others.

- **Functional** budgets include production budgets, marketing budgets, sales budgets, personnel budgets, purchasing budgets and research and development budgets.

- *Possible pitfalls*

  Not knowing the difference between a budget and a forecast
  Not understanding the meanings of correlation coefficient and coefficient of determination
  Forgetting that linear regression gives an *estimate* only. It is not wholly reliable.

14 Forecasting   74 mins

14.1 The following four data pairs have been obtained: (1, 5), (2, 6), (4, 9), (5, 11). Without carrying out any calculations, which of the following correlation coefficients best describes the relationship between x and y?

A −0.98   B −0.25   C 0.98   D 0.25

(2 marks)

14.2 A company's management accountant is analysing the reject rates achieved by 100 factory operatives working in identical conditions. Reject rates, Y%, are found to be related to months of experience, X, by this regression equation: $Y = 20 - 0.25X$. (The correlation coefficient was $r = -0.9$.)

Using the equation, what is the predicted reject rate for an operative with 12 months' experience?

A 17%   B 19%   C 20%   D 23%

(2 marks)

14.3 A regression equation $Y = a + bX$ is used to forecast the value of Y for a given value of X. Which of the following increase the reliability of the forecast?

(i)   A correlation coefficient numerically close to 1
(ii)   Working to a higher number of decimal places of accuracy
(iii) Forecasting for values of X outside the range of those used in the sample
(iv)   A large sample is used to calculate the regression equation

A (i) only   B (i) and (ii) only   C (i) and (iii) only   D (i) and (iv) only

(2 marks)

14.4 If $\Sigma x = 12$, $\Sigma y = 42$, $\Sigma x^2 = 46$, $\Sigma y^2 = 542$, $\Sigma xy = 157$ and $n = 4$, what is the correlation coefficient?

A 0.98   B −0.98   C 0.26   D 0.008

(2 marks)

14.5 Using data from twelve European countries, it has been calculated that the correlation between the level of car ownership and the number of road deaths is 0.73. Which of the statements shown follow from this?

(i)   High levels of car ownership cause high levels of road deaths
(ii)   There is a strong relationship between the level of car ownership and the number of road deaths
(iii) 53% of the variation in the level of road deaths from one country to the next can be explained by the corresponding variation in the level of car ownership
(iv)   73% of the variation in the level of road deaths from one country to the next can be explained by the corresponding variation in the level of car ownership

A (i) and (ii) only   B (i) and (iii) only   C (ii) and (iii) only   D (ii) and (iv) only

(2 marks)

14.6 The regression equation $Y = 3 + 2X$ has been calculated from 6 pairs of values, with X ranging from 1 to 10. The correlation coefficient is 0.8. It is estimated that Y = 43 when X = 20. Which of the following are true?

(i)   The estimate is not reliable because X is outside the range of the data
(ii)   The estimate is not reliable because the correlation is low
(iii) The estimate is reliable
(iv)   The estimate is not reliable because the sample is small

A (i) and (ii) only   B (i) and (iii) only   C (ii) and (iv) only   D (i) and (iv) only

(2 marks)

14.7 In calculating the regression equation linking two variables, the standard formulae for the regression coefficients are given in terms of X and Y. Which of the following is true?

    A   X must be the variable which will be forecast

    B   It does not matter which variable is which

    C   Y must be the dependent variable

    D   Y must be the variable shown on the vertical axis of a scatter diagram   **(2 marks)**

14.8 A company uses regression analysis to establish a total cost equation for budgeting purposes.

Data for the past four months is as follows:

Month	Total cost $'000	Quantity produced $'000
1	57.5	1.25
2	37.5	1.00
3	45.0	1.50
4	60.0	2.00
	200.0	5.75

The gradient of the regression line is 17.14.

What is the value of a?

    A   25.36

    B   48.56

    C   74.64

    D   101.45   **(2 marks)**

14.9 Regression analysis is being used to fine the line of best fit $(y = a + bx)$ from eleven pairs of data. The calculations have produced the following information:

$\Sigma x = 440$, $\Sigma y = 330$, $\Sigma x^2 = 17,986$, $\Sigma y^2 = 10,366$ and $\Sigma xy = 13,467$

What is the value of 'a' in the equation for the line of best fit (to 2 decimal places)?

    A   0.63

    B   0.69

    C   2.33

    D   5.33   **(2 marks)**

14.10 Which of the following is a feasible value for the correlation coefficient?

    A   − 2.0

    B   − 1.2

    C   0

    D   + 1.2   **(2 marks)**

14.11 Over an 18-month period, sales have been found to have an underlying linear trend of $y = 7.112 + 3.949x$, where y is the number of items sold and x represents the month. Monthly deviations from trend have been calculated and month 19 is expected to be 1.12 times the trend value.

What is the forecast number of items to be sold in month 19?

    A 91   B 92   C 93   D 94

    (2 marks)

14.12 Based on the last 15 periods the underlying trend of sales is $y = 345.12 − 1.35x$. If the 16th period has a seasonal factor of −23.62, assuming an additive forecasting model, then the forecast for that period, in whole units, is

    A 300   B 301   C 324   D   325

    (2 marks)

14.13 Unemployment numbers actually recorded in a town for the second quarter of the year 2000 were 4,700. The underlying trend at this point was 4,300 people and the seasonal factor is 0.92. Using the multiplicative model for seasonal adjustment, what is the seasonally-adjusted figure (in whole numbers) for the quarter?

A   3,932   B   3,956   C   5,068   D   5,109

(2 marks)

14.14 Monthly sales have been found to follow a linear trend of y = 9.82 + 4.372x, where y is the number of items sold and x is the number of the month. Monthly deviations from the trend have been calculated and follow an additive model. In month 24, the seasonal variation is estimated to be plus 8.5.

What is the forecast number of items to be sold in month 24? (to the nearest whole number.)

A   106   B   115   C   123   D   152

(2 marks)

14.15 Which of the following are necessary if forecasts obtained from a time series analysis are to be reliable?

1   There must be no unforeseen events
2   The model used must fit the past data
3   The trend must be increasing
4   There must be no seasonal variation

A 1 only   B 1 and 2 only   C 1, 2 and 3 only   D 1, 2, 3 and 4

(2 marks)

14.16 What is the purpose of seasonally adjusting the values in a time series?

A   To obtain an instant estimate of the degree of seasonal variation
B   To obtain an instant estimate of the trend
C   To ensure that seasonal components total zero
D   To take the first step in a time series analysis of the data   **(2 marks)**

14.17 The following data represents a time series:

X   36   Y   41   34   38   42

A series of three point moving averages produced from this data has given the first two values as 38
    39

What are the values of (X, Y) in the original time series?

A (38, 39)   B (38, 40)   C (40, 38)   D (39, 38)

(2 marks)

14.18 Using an additive time series model, the quarterly trend (Y) is given by Y = 65 + 7t, where t is the quarter (starting with t = 1 in the first quarter of 20X5). If the seasonal component in the fourth quarter is –30, forecast the actual value for the fourth quarter of 20X6, to the nearest whole number.

A 63   B 546   C 85   D 91

(2 marks)

14.19 The trend for monthly sales ($Y) is related to the month (t) by the equation Y = 1,500 – 3t where t = 1 in the first month of 20X8. The forecast sales (to the nearest pound) for the first month of 20X9 if the seasonal component for that month is 0.92 using a multiplicative model is

A $1,377   B $17,904   C $1,344   D $1,462

(2 marks)

14.20 Which of the following are necessary if forecasts obtained from a time series analysis are to be reliable?

1 The trend must not be increasing or decreasing
2 The trend must continue as in the past
3 Extrapolation must not be used
4 The same pattern of seasonal variation must continue as in the past

A I only   B I and II only   C I and III only   D I and IV only
(2 marks)

14.21 Under which of the following circumstances would a multiplicative model be preferred to an additive model in time series analysis?

A   When a model easily understood by non-accountants is required
B   When the trend is increasing or decreasing
C   When the trend is steady
D   When accurate forecasts are required
(2 marks)

14.22 In a time series analysis, the trend equation for a particular product is given by

TREND = $0.0002 \times YEAR^2 + 0.4 \times YEAR + 30.4$

Due to the cyclical factor, the forecast for the year 2000 is estimated at 1.6 times trend.

In whole units, the forecast for the year 2000 is

A 2,606   B 2,607   C 2,608   D 2,609
(2 marks)

14.23 A company's annual profits have a trend line given by Y = 20t − 10, where Y is the trend in $'000 and t is the year with t = 0 in 20X0.

What are the forecast profits for the year 20X9 using an additive model if the cyclical component for that year is −30?

A $160,000   B $140,000   C $119,000   D $60,000
(2 marks)

The following information is to be used for questions 14.24 and 14.25

In a time series analysis, the multiplicative model is used to forecast sales and the following seasonal variations apply:

Quarter	1	2	3	4
Seasonal variation	1.2	1.3	0.4	?

The actual sales values for the first two quarters of 2006 were:

Quarter 1: $125,000
Quarter 2: $130,000

14.24 What is the seasonal variation for the fourth quarter?

A   −2.9
B   0.9
C   1.0
D   1.1
(2 marks)

14.25 The trend line for sales:

A   Decreased between quarter 1 and quarter 2 .
B   Increased between quarter 1 and quarter 2.
C   Remained constant between quarter 1 and quarter 2.
D   Cannot be determined from the information given.
(2 marks)

14.26 In January, the unemployment in Ruritania is 567,800. If the seasonal factor using an additive time series model is +90,100, what is the seasonally-adjusted level of unemployment (to the nearest whole number)?

A 90,100   B 477,700   C 567,800   D 657,900

(2 marks)

14.27 The following statements relate to Paasche and Laspeyre indices.

(i)   Constructing a Paasche index is generally more costly than a Laspeyre index

(ii) With a Laspeyre index, comparisons can only be drawn directly between the current year and the base year

Which statements are true?

A   Both statements are true
B   Both statements are false
C   (i) is true and (ii) is false
D   (ii) is true and (i) is false

(2 marks)

14.28 The following information is available for the price of materials used at P Co.

Laspeyre index for price in 20X5 (with base year of 20X0):   150.0
Corresponding Paasche index   138.24

Calculate Fisher's ideal index.

A   12.00
B   16.98
C   144.00
D   288.24

(2 marks)

14.29 A large bag of cement cost $0.80 in 20X3. The price indices are as follows.

20X3   91
20X4   95
20X5   103
20X6   106

How much does a bag of cement cost in 20X6?

A $0.69
B $0.85
C $0.92
D $0.95

(2 marks)

14.30 Four years ago material X cost $5 per kg and the price index most appropriate to the cost of material X stood at 150.

The same index now stands at 430.

What is the best estimate of the current cost of material X per kg?

A $1.74 ($5 × 150 ÷ 430)
B $9.33 ($5 × (430 − 150) ÷ 150
C $14.33 ($5 × 430 ÷ 150)
D $21.50 ($5 × 430 ÷ 100)

(2 marks)

14.31 Six years ago material M cost $10 per kg and the price index most appropriate to the cost of material M was 130. The same index now stands at 510.

What is the best estimate of the current cost of material M per kg?

A $2.55
B $29.23
C $39.23
D $51.00 **(2 marks)**

(Total = 62 marks)

---

15 Budgeting

24 mins

15.1 Which of the following may be considered to be objectives of budgeting?

(i) Co-ordination
(ii) Communication
(iii) Expansion
(iv) Resource allocation

A All of them
B (i), (ii) and (iv)
C (ii), (iii) and (iv)
D (ii) and (iv) **(2 marks)**

15.2 What does the statement 'sales is the principal budget factor' mean?

A The level of sales will determine the level of cash at the end of the period
B The level of sales will determine the level of profit at the end of the period
C The company's activities are limited by the level of sales it can achieve
D Sales is the largest item in the budget **(2 marks)**

15.3 Which of the following tasks would usually be carried out first in the budgetary planning process?

A Identify the principal budget factor
B Establish the level of sales demand
C Calculate the predetermined overhead absorption rate
D Establish the organisation's long term objectives **(2 marks)**

15.4 QT Co manufactures a single product and an extract from their flexed budget for production costs is as follows.

	Activity level	
	80%	90%
	$	$
Direct material	2,400	2,700
Labour	2,120	2,160
Production overhead	4,060	4,080
	8,580	8,940

What would the total production cost allowance be in a budget flexed at the 83% level of activity? (to the nearest $)

A $6,266
B $6,888
C $8,586
D $8,688 **(2 marks)**

15.5 Which of these statements is untrue?

  A   Spreadsheets make the calculation and manipulation of data easier and quicker.
  B   Spreadsheets are very useful for word-processing
  C   Budgeting can be done very easily using spreadsheets
  D   Spreadsheets are useful for plotting graphs   **(2 marks)**

The following data applies to questions 15.6 to 15.7:

	A	B	C	D	F	G
1		Jan	Feb	Mar	Apr	May
2	Sales	15,000	13,400	16,100	17,200	15,300
3	Cost of sales	11,090	10,060	12,040	13,000	11,100
4	Gross profit	3,910	3,340	4,060	4,200	4,200
5	Expenses	1,500	1,500	1,500	1,500	1,500
6	Net profit	2,410	1,840	2,560	2,700	2,700
7						
8	Net profit %					

15.6 The formula =C2-C3 will give the contents of which cell?

  A   C6
  B   C4
  C   C5
  D   C1   **(2 marks)**

15.7 What would be the formula for March net profit?

  A   =D2-D3
  B   =B6+C6
  C   =D4-D5
  D   =D3*D8   **(2 marks)**

15.8 What will be the formula to go in G8?

  A   =G6/G2*100
  B   =G4/100*G6
  C   =G2/G6*100
  D   =G6/G4*100   **(2 marks)**

15.9 A company manufactures a single product. In a computer spreadsheet the cells F1 to F12 contain the budgeted monthly sales units for the twelve months of next year in sequence, with January sales in cell F1 and finishing with December sales in F12. The company policy is for the closing inventory of finished goods each month to be 10% of the budgeted sales units for the following month.

  Which of the following formulae will generate the budgeted production (in units) for March next year?

  A   =[F3 + (0.1*F4)]
  B   =[F3 – (0.1*F4)]
  C   =[(1.1*F3) – (0.1*F4)]
  D   =[(0.9*F3) + (0.1*F4)]   **(2 marks)**

15.10 Which of the following are disadvantages of flexible budgets?

  1   They are not very useful for decision-making
  2   They are more time consuming to prepare than fixed budgets
  3   They fail to provide an appropriate yardstick for cost control purposes
  4   They are based on a set of assumptions which may be over simplistic

  A   2 and 4 only
  B   2, 3 and 4 only
  C   1, 2 and 3 only
  D   1, 3 and 4 only   **(2 marks)**

(Total = 20 marks)

16 The budgetary process   34 mins

16.1 A master budget comprises

   A   the budgeted income statement
   B   the budgeted cash flow, budgeted income statement and budgeted statement of financial position
   C   the budgeted cash flow
   D   the entire set of budgets prepared   **(2 marks)**

16.2 Which of the following is **not** a functional budget?

   A   Production budget
   B   Distribution cost budget
   C   Selling cost budget
   D   Cash budget   **(2 marks)**

16.3 If a company has no production resource limitations, in which order would the following budgets be prepared?

   1   Material usage budget   4   Finished goods inventory budget
   2   Sales budget   5   Production budget
   3   Material purchase budget   6   Material inventory budget

   A   5, 4, 1, 6, 3, 2
   B   2, 4, 5, 1, 6, 3
   C   2, 4, 5, 1, 3, 6
   D   2, 5, 4, 1, 6, 3   **(2 marks)**

16.4 In a situation where there are no production resource limitations, which of the following items of information must be available for the production budget to be completed?

   1   Sales volume from the sales budget
   2   Material purchases from the purchases budget
   3   Budgeted change in finished goods inventory
   4   Standard direct labour cost per unit

   A   1, 2 and 3
   B   1, 3 and 4
   C   1 and 3
   D   All of them   **(2 marks)**

16.5 When preparing a production budget, the quantity to be produced equals

   A   sales quantity + opening inventory of finished goods + closing inventory of finished goods
   B   sales quantity – opening inventory of finished goods + closing inventory of finished goods
   C   sales quantity – opening inventory of finished goods – closing inventory of finished goods
   D   sales quantity + opening inventory of finished goods – closing inventory of finished goods
                                                                            (2 marks)

16.6 The quantity of material in the material purchases budget is greater than the inferred from quantity of material in the material usage budget. Which of the following statements can be this situation?

   A   Wastage of material occurs in the production process
   B   Finished goods inventories are budgeted to increase
   C   Raw materials inventories are budgeted to increase
   D   Raw materials inventories are budgeted to decrease   **(2 marks)**

16.7 A company plans to sell 24,000 units of product R next year. Opening inventory of R is expected to be 2,000 units and PQ Co plans to increase inventory by 25 per cent by the end of the year. How many units of product R should be produced next year?

   A   23,500 units
   B   24,000 units
   C   24,500 units
   D   30,000 units   **(2 marks)**

16.8 Each unit of product Alpha requires 3 kg of raw material. Next month's production budget for product Alpha is as follows.

Opening inventories:

Raw materials	15,000 kg
Finished units of Alpha	2,000 units
Budgeted sales of Alpha	60,000 units

Planned closing inventories:

Raw materials	7,000 kg
Finished units of Alpha	3,000 units

The number of kilograms of raw materials that should be purchased next month is:

A   172,000
B   175,000
C   183,000
D   191,000   **(2 marks)**

16.9 Budgeted sales of X for December are 18,000 units. At the end of the production process for X, 10% of production units are scrapped as defective. Opening inventories of X for December are budgeted to be 15,000 units and closing inventories will be 11,400 units. All inventories of finished goods must have successfully passed the quality control check. The production budget for X for December, in units is

A   12,960
B   14,400
C   15,840
D   16,000   **(2 marks)**

16.10 A company manufactures a single product, M. Budgeted production output of product M during August is 200 units. Each unit of product M requires 6 labour hours for completion and PR Co anticipates 20 per cent idle time. Labour is paid at a rate of $7 per hour. The direct labour cost budget for August is

A $6,720   C $10,080
B $8,400   D $10,500   **(2 marks)**

16.11 Each unit of product Echo takes five direct labour hours to make. Quality standards are high, and 8% of units are rejected after completion as sub-standard. Next month's budgets are as follows.

Opening inventories of finished goods	3,000 units
Planned closing inventories of finished goods	7,600 units
Budgeted sales of Echo	36,800 units

All inventories of finished goods must have successfully passed the quality control check.

What is the direct labour hours budget for the month?

A   190,440 hours
B   207,000 hours
C   223,560 hours
D   225,000 hours   **(2 marks)**

16.12 Budgeted production in a factory for next period is 4,800 units. Each unit requires five labour hours to make. Labour is paid $10 per hour. Idle time represents 20% of the total labour time.

What is the budgeted total labour cost for the next period?

A $192,000   C $288,000
B $240,000   D $300,000   **(2 marks)**

16.13 Which of the following statements are true?

1   A flexible budget allows businesses to evaluate a manager's performance more fairly
2   A fixed budget is useful for defining the broad objectives of the organisation
3   Relying on fixed budgets alone would usually give rise to massive variances

A   1 and 3 only
B   1 and 2 only
C   2 and 3 only
D   1, 2 and 3   (2 marks)

16.14 Which of the following statements are true?

1   Flexed budgets help managers to deal with uncertainty
2   Flexed budgets allow a more meaningful comparison to the made with actual results

A   1 is true and 2 is false
B   2 is true and 1 is false
C   1 and 2 are true
D   1 and 2 are false   (2 marks)

(Total = 28 marks)

17   Making budgets work   14 mins

17.1   Participation by staff in the budgeting process is often seen as an aid to the creation of a realistic budget
       and to the motivation of staff. There are, however, limitations to the effectiveness of such participation.

       Which of the following illustrates one of these limitations

       A   Participation allows staff to buy into the budget
       B   Staff suggestions may be ignored leading to de-motivation
       C   Staff suggestions may be based on local knowledge
       D   Budgetary slack can be built in by senior manager as well as staff   (2 marks)

17.2   Which of the following statements about budgeting and motivation are true?

       1   A target is more motivating than no target at all
       2   The problem with a target is setting an appropriate degree of difficulty
       3   Employees who are challenged tend to withdraw their commitment

       A   All of them
       B   2 and 3 only
       C   1 and 2 only
       D   3 only   (2 marks)

17.3   Which of the following best describes a top-down budget?

       A   A budget which has been set by scaling down individual expenditure items until the total
            budgeted expenditure can be met from available resources

       B   A budget which is set by delegating authority from top management, allowing budget holders to
            participate in setting their own budgets

       C   A budget which is set without permitting the ultimate budget holder to participate in the
            budgeting process

       D   A budget which is set within the framework of strategic plans determined by top management
                                                                                    (2 marks)

17.4 In which of the following situations are imposed budgets effective?

    A   In large businesses
    B   During periods of economic boom
    C   In well established businesses
    D   When the organisation's different units require precise organisation   **(2 marks)**

17.5 In which of the following circumstances are participative budgets effective?

    1   In decentralised organisations
    2   During periods of economic affluence
    3   When an organisation's different units act autonomously

    A   All of them
    B   2 and 3 only
    C   1 and 2 only
    D   3 only   **(2 marks)**

17.6 Which of the following best describes a controllable cost?

    A   A cost which can be easily forecast and is therefore readily controllable using budgetary control techniques
    B   A cost which can be specifically identified with a particular cost object
    C   A cost which is easily controlled because it is not affected by fluctuations in the level of activity
    D   A cost which can be influenced by its budget holder   **(2 marks)**

(Total = 12 marks)

Do you know? – Capital investment appraisal

Check that you can fill in the blanks in the statements below before you attempt any questions. If in doubt, you should go back to your BPP Interactive Text and revise first.

- The basic principle of .... involves calculating the present value of an investment. The present value of an investment is the amount of money which must be invested now (for a number of years) in order to earn a future sum (at a given rate of interest).

- A constant sum of money received or paid each year for a given number of years is known as an .... If this constant sum lasts forever, then it is known as a ....

- Annuity x annuity factor = ...

- Annuity ÷ interest rate = ...

- The two main discounted cash flow methods ──┌── NPV
  └── IRR

  - **Net present value (NPV) method**. If an investment has a .... NPV then it is acceptable. An investment with a .... NPV should be rejected.

  - **Internal rate of return (IRR) method**. This method determines the rate of interest at which the NPV of the investment = ... The project is viable if the IRR exceeds the minimum acceptable return.

- The IRR formula is as follows.

$$IRR = a\% + \left[\frac{A}{A-B} \times (b-a) \right]\%$$

Where
a = ...
b = ...
A = ...
B = ...

- The time that is required for the cash inflows from a capital investment project to equal the cash outflows is known as the ....

- *Possible pitfalls*

  Write down the mistakes you know you should avoid.

Did you know? – Capital investment appraisal

Could you fill in the blanks? The answers are in bold. Use this page for revision purposes as you approach the exam.

- The basic principle of **discounting** involves calculating the present value of an investment. The present value of an investment is the amount of money which must be invested now (for a number of years) in order to earn a future sum (at a given rate of interest).

- A constant sum of money received or paid each year for a given number of years is known as an **annuity**. If this constant sum lasts forever, then it is known as a **perpetuity**.

- Annuity x annuity factor = **present value of an annuity**

- Annuity ÷ interest rate = **present value of a perpetuity**

- The two main discounted cash flow methods ⎯⎡⎯ NPV
⎣⎯ IRR

  - **Net present value (NPV) method**. If an investment has a **positive** NPV then it is acceptable. An investment with a **negative** NPV should be rejected.

  - **Internal rate of return (IRR) method**. This method determines the rate of interest at which the NPV of the investment = **zero**. The project is viable if the IRR exceeds the minimum acceptable return.

- The IRR formula is as follows.

$$IRR = a\% + \left[\frac{A}{A-B} \times (b-a)\right]\%$$

  Where   a = **one interest rate**

                   b = **the other interest rate**

                   A = **NPV at rate a**

                   B = **NPV at rate b**

- The time that is required for the cash inflows from a capital investment project to equal the cash outflows is known as the **payback period**.

- *Possible pitfalls*

  - Not being able to calculate and distinguish between the nominal rate of interest and the effective annual rate of interest

  - Not being able to calculate the IRR of an investment, even when given the IRR formula. (You must remember what the symbols in the formula mean so that you can use the correct figures in your calculations.)

18   Capital expenditure budgeting   10 mins

18.1   You are currently employed as a Management Accountant in an insurance company. You are contemplating starting your own business. In considering whether or not to start your own business, your current salary level would be:

    A   A sunk cost   C   An irrelevant cost
    B   An incremental cost   D   An opportunity cost   **(2 marks)**

18.2   In decision making, costs which need to be considered are said to be relevant costs. Which of the following are characteristics associated with relevant costs?

    1   Future costs
    2   Unavoidable costs
    3   Incremental costs
    4   Differential costs

    A   1 and 3 only
    B   1 and 2 only
    C   1, 3 and 4 only
    D   All of them   **(2 marks)**

18.3   A machine owned by a company has been idle for some months but could now be used on a one year contract which is under consideration. The net book value of the machine is $1,000. If not used on this contract, the machine could be sold now for a net amount of $1,200. After use on the contract, the machine would have no saleable value and the cost of disposing of it in one year's time would be $800.

What is the total relevant cost of the machine to the contract?

    A $400   C $1,200
    B $800   D $2,000   **(2 marks)**

18.4   Which of the following would be part of the capital expenditure budget?

    1   Purchase of a new factory premises
    2   Replacement of existing machinery
    3   Refurbishment of existing factory premises
    4   Purchases of raw materials

    A   1 and 2 only   B   3 and 4 only
    C   1, 2 and 3 only   D   2 and 4 only   **(2 marks)**

(Total = 8 marks)

19   Methods of project appraisal   55 mins

19.1   A building society adds interest monthly to investors' accounts even though interest rates are expressed in annual terms. The current rate of interest is 6% per annum.

An investor deposits $1,000 on 1 January. How much interest will have been earned by 30 June?

    A $30.00
    B $30.38
    C $60.00
    D $300   **(2 marks)**

19.2   A one-year investment yields a return of 15%. The cash returned from the investment, including principal and interest, is $2,070. The interest is

    A $250
    B $270
    C $300
    D $310.50   **(2 marks)**

19.3   If a single sum of $12,000 is invested at 8% per annum with interest compounded quarterly, the amount to which the principal will have grown by the end of year three is approximately

    A $15,117
    B $9,528
    C $15,219
    D $30,924   **(2 marks)**

19.4   Which is worth most, at present values, assuming an annual rate of interest of 8%?

    A $1,200 in exactly one year from now
    B $1,400 in exactly two years from now
    C $1,600 in exactly three years from now
    D $1,800 in exactly four years from now   **(2 marks)**

19.5   A bank offers depositors a nominal 4% pa, with interest payable quarterly. What is the effective annual rate of interest?

    A   1%
    B   4%
    C   1.025%
    D   4.06%   **(2 marks)**

19.6   A project requiring an investment of $1,200 is expected to generate returns of $400 in years 1 and 2 and $350 in years 3 and 4. If the NPV = $22 at 9% and the NPV = –$4 at 10%, what is the IRR for the project?

    A   9.15%
    B   9.85%
    C   10.15%
    D   10.85%   **(2 marks)**

19.7   A sum of money was invested for 10 years at 7% per annum and is now worth $2,000. The original amount invested (to the nearest $) was

    A $1,026
    B $1,016
    C $3,937
    D $14,048   **(2 marks)**

19.8 House prices rise at 2% per calendar month. The annual rate of increase correct to one decimal place is

    A   24%
    B   26.8%
    C   12.7%
    D   12.2%   **(2 marks)**

19.9 Find the present value of ten annual payments of $700, the first paid immediately and discounted at 8%, giving your answer to the nearest $.

    A $4,697
    B $1,050
    C $4,435
    D $5,073   **(2 marks)**

19.10 An investor is to receive an annuity of $19,260 for six years commencing at the end of year 1. It has a present value of $86,400.

The rate of interest (to the nearest whole percent) is

    A   4%
    B   7%
    C   9%
    D   11%   **(2 marks)**

19.11 How much should be invested now (to the nearest $) to receive $24,000 per annum in perpetuity if the annual rate of interest is 5%?

    A $1,200
    B $25,200
    C $120,000
    D $480,000   **(2 marks)**

19.12 The net present value of an investment at 12% is $24,000, and at 20% is –$8,000. What is the internal rate of return of this investment?

    A   6%
    B   12%
    C   16%
    D   18%   **(2 marks)**

State your answer to the nearest whole percent.

The following data is relevant for questions 19.13 and 19.14

Diamond Ltd has a payback period limit of three years and is considering investing in one of the following projects. Both projects require an initial investment of $800,000. Cash inflows accrue evenly throughout the year.

Project Alpha			Project Beta	
Year	Cash inflow $		Year	Cash inflow $
1	250,000		1	250,000
2	250,000		2	350,000
3	400,000		3	400,000
4	300,000		4	200,000
5	200,000		5	150,000
6	50,000		6	150,000

The company's cost of capital is 10%.

19.13 What is the non-discounted payback period of Project Beta?

A   2 years and 2 months
B   2 years and 4 months
C   2 years and 5 months
D   2 years and 6 months   **(2 marks)**

19.14 What is the discounted payback period of Project Alpha?

A   Between 1 and 2 years
B   Between 3 and 4 years
C   Between 4 and 5 years
D   Between 5 and 6 years   **(2 marks)**

19.15 A capital investment project has an initial investment followed by constant annual returns.

How is the payback period calculated?

A   Initial investment ÷ annual profit
B   Initial investment ÷ annual net cash inflow
C   (Initial investment – residual value) ÷ annual profit
D   (Initial investment – residual value) ÷ annual net cash inflow   **(2 marks)**

19.16 A machine has an investment cost of $60,000 at time 0. The present values (at time 0) of the expected net cash inflows from the machine over its useful life are:

Discount rate	Present value of cash inflows
10%	$64,600
15%	$58,200
20%	$52,100

What is the internal rate of return (IRR) of the machine investment?

A   Below 10%
B   Between 10% and 15%
C   Between 15% and 20%
D   Over 20%   **(2 marks)**

19.17 An investment project has a positive net present value (NPV) of $7,222 when its cash flows are discounted at the cost of capital of 10% per annum. Net cash inflows from the project are expected to be $18,000 per annum for five years. The cumulative discount (annuity) factor for five years at 10% is 3.791.

What is the investment at the start of the project?

A $61,016
B $68,238
C $75,460
D $82,778   **(2 marks)**

19.18 The following statements relate to an investment project that has been discounted at rates of 10% and 20%:

1. The discounted payback period at 10% will be longer than the discounted payback period at 20%.

2. The discounted payback period at 20% will be longer than the discounted payback period at 10%.

3. The non-discounted payback period will be longer than the discounted payback period.

4. The non-discounted payback period will be shorter than the discounted payback period.

Which of the statements are true?

A 1 and 3
B 1 and 4
C 2 and 3
D 2 and 4 **(2 marks)**

19.19 Which of the following accurately defines the internal rate of return (IRR)?

A The average annual profit from an investment expressed as a percentage of the investment sum

B The discount rate (%) at which the net present value of the cash flows from an investment is zero

C The net present value of the cash flows from an investment discounted at the required rate of return

D The rate (%) at which discounted net profits from an investment are zero **(2 marks)**

19.20 An investment project has the following discounted cash flows ($'000):

Year		Discount rate	
	0%	10%	20%
0	(90)	(90)	(90)
1	30	27.3	25.0
2	30	24.8	29.8
3	30	22.5	17.4
4	30	20.5	14.5
	30	5.1	(12.3)

The required rate of return on investment is 10% per annum.

What is the discounted payback period of the investment project?

A Less than 3.0 years
B 3.0 years
C Between 3.0 years and 4.0 years
D More than 4.0 years **(2 marks)**

19.21 What is the effective annual rate of interest of 2.1% compounded every three months?

A 6.43%
B 8.40%
C 8.67%
D 10.87% **(2 marks)**

19.22 If the interest rate is 8%, what would you pay for a perpetuity of $1,500 starting in one year's time? (to the nearest $)

A $1,620
B $17,130
C $18,750
D $20,370 **(2 marks)**

19.23 How much should be invested now (to the nearest $) to receive $24,000 per annum in perpetuity if the annual rate of interest is 5%?

    A $1,200
    B $478,800
    C $480,000
    D $481,200   **(2 marks)**

(Total = 46 marks)

Do you know? – Standard costing

Check that you can fill in the blanks in the statements below before you attempt any questions. If in doubt, you should go back to your BPP Interactive Text and revise first.

- If an organisation uses standard marginal costing instead of standard absorption costing, there will be no .... variance and the ..../............ /............ variances will be valued at the standard contribution per unit (as opposed to standard profit per unit).

- There are many possible reasons for variances arising including efficiencies and inefficiencies of operations, errors in standard setting and changes in exchange rates.

- Individual variances should not be looked at in isolation. They might be interdependent/ interrelated. One may be .... and one ....

- An .... provides a reconciliation between budgeted and actual profit.

- .... , ... and .... should be considered before a decision about whether or not to investigate a variance is taken. One way of deciding whether or not to investigate a variance is to investigate only those variances which exceed pre-set tolerance limits.

- A variance should only be investigated if the expected value of .... from investigation and any control action exceed the ....of investigation.

- If the cause of a variance is controllable, action can be taken to bring the system back under control in future. If the variance is uncontrollable, but not simply due to chance, it will be necessary to review .... of expected results, and perhaps to revise the ....

- *Possible pitfalls*

  Write down a list of mistakes you know you should avoid.

Did you know? – Standard costing

Could you fill in the blanks? The answers are in bold. Use this page for revision purposes as you approach the exam.

- If an organisation uses standard marginal costing instead of standard absorption costing, there will be no **fixed overhead volume** variance and the **sales volume/quantity/mix** variances will be valued at the standard contribution per unit (as opposed to standard profit per unit).

- There are many possible reasons for variances arising including efficiencies and inefficiencies of operations, errors in standard setting and changes in exchange rates.

- Individual variances should not be looked at in isolation. They might be interdependent/ interrelated. One may be **adverse** and one **favourable**.

- An **operating statement** provides a reconciliation between budgeted and actual profit.

- **Materiality, controllability** and **variance trend** should be considered before a decision about whether or not to investigate a variance is taken. One way of deciding whether or not to investigate a variance is to investigate only those variances which exceed pre-set tolerance limits.

- A variance should only be investigated if the expected value of **benefits** from investigation and any control action exceed the **costs** of investigation.

- If the cause of a variance is controllable, action can be taken to bring the system back under control in future. If the variance is uncontrollable, but not simply due to chance, it will be necessary to review **forecasts** of expected results, and perhaps to revise the **budget**.

- *Possible pitfalls*

    - Forgetting to state whether the variance is adverse or favourable
    - Not learning how to calculate each type of variance.

20 Standard costing   17 mins

20.1 A company is in the process of setting standard unit costs for next period. Product J uses two types of material, P and S. 7 kg of material P and 3 kg of material S are needed, at a standard price of $4 per kg and $9 per kg respectively.

Direct labour will cost $7 per hour and each unit of J requires 5 hours of labour.

Production overheads are to be recovered at the rate of $6 per direct labour hour, and general overhead is to be absorbed at a rate of ten per cent of production cost.

The standard prime cost for one unit of product J will be:

A $55   B $90   C $120   D $132

(2 marks)

20.2 What is an attainable standard?

A   A standard which includes no allowance for losses, waste and inefficiencies. It represents the level of performance which is attainable under perfect operating conditions

B   A standard which includes some allowance for losses, waste and inefficiencies. It represents the level of performance which is attainable under efficient operating conditions

C   A standard which is based on currently attainable operating conditions

D   A standard which is kept unchanged, to show the trend in costs   (2 marks)

20.3 Which of the following statements is correct?

A   The operating standards set for production should be the most ideal possible.

B   The operating standards set for production should be the minimal level.

C   The operating standards set for production should be the attainable level.

D   The operating standards set for production should be the maximum level.   (2 marks)

20.4 A company manufactures a carbonated drink, which is sold in 1 litre bottles. During the bottling process there is a 20% loss of liquid input due to spillage and evaporation. The standard usage of liquid per bottle is

A   0.80 litres   C   1.20 litres

B   1.00 litres   D   1.25 litres   (2 marks)

20.5 Which of the following best describes management by exception?

A   Using management reports to highlight exceptionally good performance, so that favourable results can be built upon to improve future outcomes.

B   Sending management reports only to those managers who are able to act on the information contained within the reports.

C   Focusing management reports on areas which require attention and ignoring those which appear to be performing within acceptable limits.

D   Focusing management reports on areas which are performing just outside acceptable limits.

(2 marks)

20.6 Standard costing provides which of the following?

1   Targets and measures of performance
2   Information for budgeting
3   Simplification of inventory control systems
4   Actual future costs

A   1, 2 and 3 only
B   2, 3 and 4 only
C   1, 3 and 4 only
D   1, 2 and 4 only   (2 marks)

20.7 A unit of product L requires 9 active labour hours for completion. The performance standard for product L allows for ten per cent of total labour time to be idle, due to machine downtime. The standard wage rate is $9 per hour. What is the standard labour cost per unit of product L?

    A $72.90
    B $81.00
    C $89.10
    D $90.00   (2 marks)

                                                                    (Total = 14 marks)

21 Basic variance analysis   46 mins

21.1 A company manufactures a single product L, for which the standard material cost is as follows.

                                                        $ per unit
    Material 14 kg × $3   42

    During July, 800 units of L were manufactured, 12,000 kg of material were purchased for $33,600, of which 11,500 kg were issued to production.

    SM Co values all inventory at standard cost.

    The material price and usage variances for July were:

	Price	Usage
A	$2,300 (F)	$900 (A)
B	$2,300 (F)	$300 (A)
C	$2,400 (F)	$900 (A)
D	$2,400 (F)	$840 (A)

                                                                                (2 marks)

The following information relates to questions 21.2 and 21.3

A company expected to produce 200 units of its product, the Bone, in 20X3. In fact 260 units were produced. The standard labour cost per unit was $70 (10 hours at a rate of $7 per hour). The actual labour cost was $18,600 and the labour force worked 2,200 hours although they were paid for 2,300 hours.

21.2 What is the direct labour rate variance for the company in 20X3?

    A $400 (A)   C $2,500 (A)
    B $2,500 (F)   D $3,200 (A)   (2 marks)

21.3 What is the direct labour efficiency variance for the company in 20X3?

    A $400 (A)
    B $2,100 (F)
    C $2,800 (A)
    D $2,800 (F)   (2 marks)

21.4 Extracts from a company's records from last period are as follows.

	Budget	Actual
Production	1,925 units	2,070 units
Variable production overhead cost	$11,550	$14,904
Labour hours worked	5,775	8,280

    The variable production overhead variances for last period are:

	Expenditure	Efficiency
A	$1,656 (F)	$2,070 (A)
B	$1,656 (F)	$3,726 (A)
C	$1,656 (F)	$4,140 (A)
D	$3,354 (A)	$4,140 (A)

                                                                                (2 marks)

21.5 A company has budgeted to make and sell 4,200 units of product X during the period.

The standard fixed overhead cost per unit is $4.

During the period covered by the budget, the actual results were as follows.

Production and sales	5,000 units
Fixed overhead incurred	$17,500

The fixed overhead variances for the period were

	Fixed overhead expenditure variance	Fixed overhead volume variance
A	$700 (F)	$3,200 (F)
B	$700 (F)	$3,200 (A)
C	$700 (A)	$3,200 (F)
D	$700 (A)	$3,200 (A)

(2 marks)

21.6 A company manufactures a single product, and relevant data for December is as follows.

	Budget/standard	Actual
Production units	1,800	1,900
Labour hours	9,000	9,400
Fixed production overhead	$36,000	$39,480

The fixed production overhead capacity and efficiency variances for December are:

	Capacity	Efficiency
A	$1,600 (F)	$400 (F)
B	$1,600 (A)	$400 (A)
C	$1,600 (A)	$400 (F)
D	$1,600 (F)	$400 (A)

(2 marks)

21.7 Which of the following would help to explain a favourable direct labour efficiency variance?

1 Employees were of a lower skill level than specified in the standard
2 Better quality material was easier to process
3 Suggestions for improved working methods were implemented during the period

A 1, 2 and 3
B 1 and 2 only
C 2 and 3 only
D 1 and 3 only

(2 marks)

21.8 Which of the following statements is correct?

A An adverse direct material cost variance will always be a combination of an adverse material price variance and an adverse material usage variance
B An adverse direct material cost variance will always be a combination of an adverse material price variance and a favourable material usage variance
C An adverse direct material cost variance can be a combination of a favourable material price variance and a favourable material usage variance
D An adverse direct material cost variance can be a combination of a favourable material price variance and an adverse material usage variance

(2 marks)

The following information relates to Questions 21.9 and 21.10

A company has a budgeted material cost of $125,000 for the production of 25,000 units per month. Each unit is budgeted to use 2 kg of material. The standard cost of material is $2.50 per kg.

Actual materials in the month cost $136,000 for 27,000 units and 53,000 kg were purchased and used.

21.9   What was the adverse material price variance?

    A $1,000
    B $3,500
    C $7,500
    D $11,000   **(2 marks)**

21.10   What was the favourable material usage variance?

    A $2,500
    B $4,000
    C $7,500
    D $10,000   **(2 marks)**

The following information relates to questions 21.11 and 21.12

A company operating a standard costing system has the following direct labour standards per unit for one of its products:

4 hours at $12.50 per hour

Last month when 2,195 units of the product were manufactured, the actual direct labour cost for the 9,200 hours worked was $110,750.

21.11   What was the direct labour rate variance for last month?

    A $4,250 favourable
    B $4,250 adverse
    C $5,250 favourable
    D $5,250 adverse   **(2 marks)**

21.12   What was the direct labour efficiency variance for last month?

    A $4,250 favourable
    B $4,250 adverse
    C $5,250 favourable
    D $5,250 adverse   **(2 marks)**

21.13   The following information relates to labour costs for the past month:

Budget		
	Labour rate	*$10 per hour*
	Production time	15,000 hours
	Time per unit	3 hours
	Production units	5,000 units
Actual	Wages paid	$176,000
	Production	5,500 units
	Total hours worked	14,000 hours

There was no idle time

What were the labour rate and efficiency variances?

	Rate variance	Efficiency variance
A	$26,000 adverse	$25,000 favourable
B	$26,000 adverse	$10,000 favourable
C	$36,000 adverse	$2,500 favourable
D	$36,000 adverse	$25,000 favourable

       (2 marks)

21.14 A manufacturing company operates a standard absorption costing system. Last month 25,000 production hours were budgeted and the budgeted fixed production overhead cost was $125,000. Last month the actual hours worked were 24,000 and the standard hours for actual production were 27,000.

What was the fixed production overhead capacity variance for last month?

A $5,000 Adverse
B $5,000 Favourable
C $10,000 Adverse
D $10,000 Favourable   (2 marks)

The following information relates to questions 21.15 to 21.17

Number of units produced	2,200	2,000
	Budget	*Actual*
Direct materials	$	$
	110,000	110,000
Direct labour	286,000	280,000
Variable overhead	132,000	120,000

The actual number of units produced was 2,000.

21.15 What was the total direct materials variance?

A   Nil
B $10,000 Adverse
C $10,000 Favourable
D $11,000 Adverse   (2 marks)

21.16 What was the total direct labour variance?

A $6,000 Favourable
B $20,000 Adverse
C $22,000 Favourable
D   Nil   (2 marks)

21.17 What was the total direct variable overheads variance?

A   Nil
B $12,000 Favourable
C $12,000 Adverse
D $11,000 Adverse   (2 marks)

21.18 Which of the following statements are true?

1   A favourable fixed overhead volume capacity variance occurs when actual hours of work are greater than budgeted hours of work

2   A labour force that produces 5,000 standard hours of work in 5,500 actual hours will give a favourable fixed overhead volume efficiency variance

A   1 is true and 2 is false
B   Both are true
C   Both are false
D   1 is false and 2 is true   (2 marks)

21.19 Which of the following statements are true?

    1   The fixed overhead volume capacity variance represents part of the over/under absorption of overheads

    2   A company works fewer hours than budgeted. This will result in an adverse fixed overhead volume capacity variance

    A   1 is true and 2 is false
    B   Both are true
    C   Both are false
    D   1 is false and 2 is true   **(2 marks)**

(Total = 38 marks)

22   Further variance analysis   53 mins

22.1   A company currently uses a standard absorption costing system. The fixed overhead variances extracted from the operating statement for November are:

	$
Fixed production overhead expenditure variance	5,800 adverse
Fixed production overhead capacity variance	4,200 favourable
Fixed production overhead efficiency variance	1,400 adverse

PQ Limited is considering using standard marginal costing as the basis for variance reporting in future. What variance for fixed production overhead would be shown in a marginal costing operating statement for November?

    A   No variance would be shown for fixed production overhead
    B   Expenditure variance: $5,800 adverse
    C   Volume variance: $2,800 favourable
    D   Total variance: $3,000 adverse   **(2 marks)**

22.2   Which of the following situations is most likely to result in a favourable selling price variance?

    A   The sales director decided to change from the planned policy of market skimming pricing to one of market penetration pricing.

    B   Fewer customers than expected took advantage of the early payment discounts offered.

    C   Competitors charged lower prices than expected, therefore selling prices had to be reduced in order to compete effectively.

    D   Demand for the product was higher than expected and prices could be raised without adverse effects on sales volumes.   **(2 marks)**

The following information relates to questions 22.3 to 22.6

A company manufactures a single product. An extract from a variance control report together with relevant standard cost data is shown below.

Standard selling price per unit	$70
Standard direct material cost (5kg × $2 per kg)	$10 per unit
Budgeted total material cost of sales	$2,300 per month
Budgeted profit margin	$6,900 per month
Actual results for February	
Sales revenue	$15,200
Total direct material cost	$2,400
Direct material price variance	$800 adverse
Direct material usage variance	$400 favourable

There was no change in inventory levels during the month.

22.3 What was the actual production in February?

A	200 units	C	240 units
B	217 units	D	280 units

(2 marks)

22.4 What was the actual usage of direct material during February?

A	800 kg	C	1,200 kg
B	1,000 kg	D	None of these

(2 marks)

22.5 What was the selling price variance for February?

A	$120 (F)	C	$1,200 (A)
B	$900 (A)	D	$1,200 (F)

(2 marks)

22.6 What was the sales volume profit variance for February?

A	$900 (F)	C	$900 (A)
B	$1,200 (F)	D	$2,100 (A)

(2 marks)

22.7 A company uses a standard absorption costing system. The following details have been extracted from its budget for April.

Fixed production overhead cost	$48,000
Production (units)	4,800

In April the fixed production overhead cost was under absorbed by $8,000 and the fixed production overhead expenditure variance was $2,000 adverse.

The actual number of units produced was

A	3,800	C	4,800
B	4,200	D	5,800

(2 marks)

22.8 A company purchased 6,850 kgs of material at a total cost of $21,920. The material price variance was $1,370 favourable. The standard price per kg was:

A	$0.20
B	$3.00
C	$3.20
D	$3.40

(2 marks)

22.9 The following data relates to one of a company's products.

	$ per unit	$ per unit
Selling price		27.00
Variable costs	12.00	
Fixed costs	9.00	
		21.00
Profit		6.00

Budgeted sales for control period 7 were 2,400 units, but actual sales were 2,550 units. The revenue earned from these sales was $67,320.

Profit reconciliation statements are drawn up using marginal costing principles. What sales variances would be included in such a statement for period 7?

	Price	Volume
A	$1,530 (A)	$900 (F)
B	$1,530 (A)	$2,250 (F)
C	$1,530 (A)	$2,250 (A)
D	$1,530 (F)	$2,250 (F)

(2 marks)

22.10 A company uses variance analysis to control costs and revenues.

Information concerning sales is as follows:

Budgeted selling price $15 per unit
Budgeted sales units   10,000 units
Budgeted profit per unit $5 per unit

Actual sales revenue $151,500
Actual units sold   9,800 units

What is the sales volume profit variance?

A $500 favourable
B $1,000 favourable
C $1,000 adverse
D $3,000 adverse   **(2 marks)**

The following information relates to questions 22.11 and 22.12

The standard direct material cost per unit for a product is calculated as follows:

10.5 litres at $2.50 per litre

Last month the actual price paid for 12,000 litres of material used was 4% above standard and the direct material usage variance was $1,815 favourable. No stocks of material are held.

22.11 What was the adverse direct material price variance for last month?

A $1,000
B $1,200
C $1,212
D $1,260   **(2 marks)**

22.12 What was the actual production last month (in units)?

A 1,074
B 1,119
C 1,212
D 1,258   **(2 marks)**

22.13 Last month a company budgeted to sell 8,000 units at a price of $12.50 per unit. Actual sales last month were 9,000 units giving a total sales revenue of $117,000.

What was the sales price variance for last month?

A $4,000 favourable
B $4,000 adverse
C $4,500 favourable
D $4,500 adverse   **(2 marks)**

22.14 A company uses a standard absorption costing system. Last month budgeted production was 8,000 units and the standard fixed production overhead cost was $15 per unit. Actual production last month was 8,500 units and the actual fixed production overhead cost was $17 per unit.

What was the total adverse fixed production overhead variance for last month?

A $7,500
B $16,000
C $17,000
D $24.500   **(2 marks)**

22.15 A cost centre had an overhead absorption rate of $4.25 per machine hour, based on a budgeted activity level of 12,400 machine hours.

In the period covered by the budget, actual machine hours worked were 2% more than the budgeted hours and the actual overhead expenditure incurred in the cost centre was $56,389.

What was the total over or under absorption of overheads in the cost centre for the period?

A $1,054 over absorbed
B $2,635 under absorbed
C $3,689 over absorbed
D $3,689 under absorbed   **(2 marks)**

22.16 A company uses standard marginal costing. Last month the standard contribution on actual sales was $10,000 and the following variances arose:

	$
Total variable costs variance	2,000 Adverse
Sales price variance	500 Favourable
Sales volume contribution variance	1,000 Adverse

What was the actual contribution for last month?

A $7,000
B $7,500
C $8,000
D $8,500   **(2 marks)**

22.17 AD Ltd manufactures and sells a single product, E, and uses a standard absorption costing system. Standard cost and selling price details for product E are as follows.

	$ per unit
Variable cost	8
Fixed cost	2
	10
Standard profit	5
Standard selling price	15

The sales volume variance reported for last period was $9,000 adverse.

AD Ltd is considering using standard marginal costing as the basis for variance reporting in future. What would be the correct sales volume variance to be shown in a marginal costing operating statement for last period?

A $6,428 (A)
B $6,428 (F)
C $12,600 (F)
D $12,600 (A)   **(2 marks)**

22.18 When comparing the profits reported under absorption costing and marginal costing during a period when the level of inventory increased:

A   Absorption costing profits will be higher and closing inventory valuations lower than those under marginal costing.

B   Absorption costing profits will be higher and closing inventory valuations higher than those under marginal costing.

C   Marginal costing profits will be higher and closing inventory valuations lower than those under absorption costing.

D   Marginal costing profits will be higher and closing inventory valuations higher than those under absorption costing.   **(2 marks)**

22.19 PH Ltd produces a single product and currently uses absorption costing for its internal management accounting reports. The fixed production overhead absorption rate is $34 per unit. Opening inventories for the year were 100 units and closing inventories were 180 units. The company's management accountant is considering a switch to marginal costing as the inventory valuation basis.

If marginal costing were used, the marginal costing profit for the year, compared with the profit calculated by absorption costing, would be:

A $2,720 lower
B $2,720 higher
C $3,400 lower
D $3,400 higher   **(2 marks)**

The following information relates to questions 22.20 and 22.21

A company produces and sells one type of product. The details for last year were as follows:

Production and Sales

	Budget	Actual
Production (units)	26,000	26,000
Sales (units)	28,000	25,000

There was no inventory at the start of the year.

Selling price and costs

	Budget	Actual
	$	$
Selling price per unit	80	80
Variable costs per unit	60	60
Fixed production overhead	143,000	113,000
Fixed selling costs	69,000	69,000

22.20 Calculate the actual profit for the year that would be reported using marginal costing.

A $312,500
B $318,000
C $323,500
D $682,000   **(2 marks)**

22.21 Calculate the actual profit for the year that would be reported using absorption costing

A $312,500
B $318,000
C $323,500
D $682,000   **(2 marks)**

22.22 The budgeted contribution for HMF Co for June was $290,000. The following variances occurred during the month.

	$	
Fixed overhead expenditure variance	6,475	Favourable
Total direct labour variance	11,323	Favourable
Total variable overhead variance	21,665	Adverse
Selling price variance	21,875	Favourable
Fixed overhead volume variance	12,500	Adverse
Sales volume variance	36,250	Adverse
Total direct materials variance	6,335	Adverse

What was the actual contribution for the month?

A $252,923
B $258,948
C $321,052
D $327,077

(2 marks)

(Total = 44 marks)

Do you know? – Performance measurement

Check that you can fill in the blanks in the statements below before you attempt any questions. If in doubt, you should go back to your BPP Interactive Text and revise first..

- A .... is a formal statement of the business' aim. It can play an important point in the .... process. Cascading downwards from this is a hierarchy of goals and .... These may be split into operational, tactical and strategic. Cascading downwards from this are the critical success factors. A critical success factor is a performance requirement that is fundamental to competitive success. .... are quantifiable measurements which reflect the critical success factors.

- The 3 Es which are generally desirable features of organisational performance are ...., ..., and ....

- The formula for return on capital employed = (............./...................) x 100%.

  Capital employed = ... + ... + ... - ....

- The ....ratio is the standard test of liquidity and is the ratio of .... to ....

- Performance of non-profit-making organisations can be measured

  ....
  ....
  ....

- The balanced scorecard measures performance in four perspectives: ...., ..., ... and ....

- .... is a planned and positive approach to reducing expenditure. Measures should be planned programmes rather than crash programmes to cut spending levels.

- Work study is a means of raising the .... of an operating unit by the .... of work. There are two main parts to work study: .... and ....

- Value analysis considers four aspects of value: .... value, ... value, ... value and .... value

- *Possible pitfalls*

  Write down a list of mistakes you know you should avoid.

Did you know? – Performance measurement

Could you fill in the blanks? The answers are in bold. Use this page for revision purposes as you approach the exam.

- A **mission statement** is a formal statement of the business' aim. It can play an important point in the **planning** process. Cascading downwards from this is a hierarchy of goals and **objectives**. These may be split into operational, tactical and strategic. Cascading downwards from this are the critical success factors. A critical success factor is a performance requirement that is fundamental to competitive success. **Key performance indicators** are quantifiable measurements which reflect the critical success factors.

- The 3 Es which are generally desirable features of organisational performance are **economy, efficiency** and **effectiveness**.

- The formula for return on capital employed = (**profit/capital employed**) x 100%.

  Capital employed = **non-current assets** + **investments** + **current assets** – **current liabilities**

- The **current** ratio is the standard test of liquidity and is the ratio **current assets** to **current liabilities**.

  Performance of non-profit-making organisations can be measured

  In terms of inputs and outputs

  By judgement

  By comparison

- The balanced scorecard measures performance in four perspectives: **customer satisfaction**, **financial success**, **process efficiency** and **growth**

- **Cost reduction** is a planned and positive approach to reducing expenditure. Measures should be planned programmes rather than crash programmes to cut spending levels.

- Work study is a means of raising the **productivity** of an operating unit by the **reorganisation** of work. There are two main parts to work study: **method study** and **work measurement**

- Value analysis considers four aspects of value: **cost** value, **exchange** value, **use** value and **esteem** value

- *Possible pitfalls*

  - Not realising that mission statements feed into objectives which feed into critical success factors which are quantified by key performance indicators

  - Not knowing the performance measures which are appropriate for service industries

  - Not knowing the meaning of the efficiency, capacity and activity ratios

  - Not knowing the formulae for measuring profitability, liquidity and gearing

23 Performance measurement   29 mins

23.1 All of the following, except one, are sound principles for devising objectives in order to enact the corporate mission. Which is the exception?

A   They should be observable or measurable
B   They should be easily achievable
C   They should relate to a specified time period
D   They should be specific   **(2 marks)**

23.2 Which one of the following performance indicators is a financial performance measure?

A   Quality rating
B   Number of customer complaints
C   Cash flow
D   System (machine) down time   **(2 marks)**

23.3 A government body uses measures based upon the 'three Es' to the measure value for money generated by a publicly funded hospital. It considers the most important performance measure to be 'cost per successfully treated patient'.

Which of the three E's best describes the above measure?

A   Economy (A measure of cost related to input)
B   Effectiveness (A measure of output related to objectives)
C   Efficiency (A measure of output related to input)
D   Externality (Not one of the three Es)   **(2 marks)**

23.4 In order for a business's strength to have a real benefit, it has to be linked to critical success factors. What are critical success factors?

A   Factors contributing to strategic success
B   Factors necessary to match strengths to opportunities
C   Factors necessary to build on strengths
D   Factors fundamental to strategic success   **(2 marks)**

23.5 The following summarised statement of financial position is available for L Co.

	$'000	$'000
Non-current assets		31,250
Current assets		
Inventory	35,000	
Receivables	40,000	
Cash	1,250	
		107,500
EQUITY AND LIABILITIES		
Capital and reserves		47,500
Current liabilities (payables only)		60,000
		107,500

Calculate the acid test ratio.

A   0.6875
B   0.7093
C   1.2708
D   2.000   **(2 marks)**

23.6   How does setting objectives relate to the mission statement of an organisation?

    A   The mission gives managers a focus for setting objectives
    B   The mission states what the objectives are
    C   The mission has nothing to do with setting objectives
    D   The mission is decided after setting the objectives   **(2 marks)**

23.7   In general terms, which of the following elements should organisations include in their mission statements?

    1   Policies and standards of behaviour

    2   Values – a description of the culture, assumptions and beliefs regarded as important to those managing the business

    3   Profitability

    4   Strategy – the commercial logic for the business, defining the nature of the business

    A   1 and 2 only
    B   3 and 4 only
    C   1, 2 and 4 only
    D   3 and 4 only   **(2 marks)**

23.8   Which of the following short-term objectives may involve the sacrifice of longer-term objectives?

    1   Reducing training costs
    2   Increasing quality control
    3   Increasing capital expenditure projects
    4   Recruiting more staff

    A   1 only
    B   1, 2 and 3 only
    C   2, 3 and 4 only
    D   4 only   **(2 marks)**

23.9   Which of the following statements are true?

    1   Non-financial performance indicators are less likely to be manipulated than financial ones
    2   Non-financial performance indicators offer a means of counteracting short-termism.

    A   1 and 2 are true
    B   1 and 2 are false
    C   1 is true and 2 is false
    D   1 is false and 2 is true   **(2 marks)**

23.10 What is short-termism?

    A   It is when non-financial performance indicators are used for measurement
    B   It is when organisations sacrifice short term objectives
    C   It is when there is a bias towards short term rather than long term performance
    D   It is when managers' performance is measured on long term results   **(2 marks)**

23.11 Which of the following performance measures is most likely to be recorded because of government regulations?

    A   Sales growth
    B   Customer numbers
    C CO_2 emissions
    D   Return on investment   **(2 marks)**

23.12 Market conditions and economic conditions can impact on performance measurement. Which of the following statements are true?

  1   The entry of a new competitor in the market will cause a business to examine sales performance measures more closely

  2   General economic conditions can raise or lower overall demand and supply.

  A   1 and 2 are true
  B   1 and 2 are false
  C   1 is true and 2 is false
  D   1 is false and 2 is true   **(2 marks)**

                                                                        (Total = 24 marks)

24 Applications of performance measures   34 mins

24.1   The following information is available for company X.

	20X7 $	20X8 $
Profit	7,500	9,000
Sales	500,000	450,000
Capital employed	37,500	60,000

Calculate the change in ROI from 20X7 to 20X8.

  A   Decrease from 20% to 15%
  B   Increase from 1.5% to 2%
  C   Increase from 7.5% to 13.3%
  D   Decrease from 100% to 90%   **(2 marks)**

24.2   Using the figures in the question above, calculate the asset turnover for 20X8.

  A   0.075 times
  B   0.13 times
  C   7.5 times
  D   13.3 times   **(2 marks)**

24.3   The usefulness of profit as a single control measure has been criticised in recent years. Which of the following is **not** a reason to support this criticism?

  A   Profit provides a narrow focus for performance measurement
  B   Profit measurement alone can lead to short-termism
  C   Profit is simple to understand
  D   Profit can be easily manipulated   **(2 marks)**

24.4   In not-for-profit businesses and state-run entities, a value-for-money audit can be used to measure performance. It covers three key areas: economy, efficiency and effectiveness. Which of the following could be used to describe effectiveness in this context?

  A   Avoiding waste of inputs
  B   Achieving agreed targets
  C   Achieving a given level of profit
  D   Obtaining suitable quality inputs at the lowest price   **(2 marks)**

24.5 Balance Co is looking to introduce a balanced scorecard and is finalising the measures to use for the 'innovation and learning' perspective. Which one of the following is not really suitable for this perspective?

A   Number of ideas from staff
B   Percentage of sales from new products
C   Number of new products introduced
D   Level of refunds given   **(2 marks)**

24.6 Qual Co is keen to increase the use they make of non-financial performance measures in their overall performance measurement activities. In particular, they are keen to improve customer retention and so want to focus on the quality of service they provide to their customers. Which of the following measures would be directly appropriate as a measure of service quality?

1   Number of customer complaints
2   Number of repeat orders as a proportion of total orders
3   Sales volume growth

A   1 and 2
B   1, 2 and 3
C   1 and 3
D   2 and 3   **(2 marks)**

24.7 Which of the following are non-financial objectives?

1   Growth of sales
2   Diversification
3   Contented workforce
4   Increase earnings per share

A   2 and 3
B   1, 2 and 3
C   2, 3 and 4
D   1, 3 and 4   **(2 marks)**

24.8 Which of the following statements about financial performance indicators are true?

1   They concentrate on too few variables
2   They give no information on quality
3   They measure success but don't help businesses to be successful

A   1 and 2
B   1 and 3
C   2 and 3
D   1, 2 and 3   **(2 marks)**

24.9 Which one of the following is not a measure of service quality?
A   Number of complaints
B   Proportion of repeat bookings
C   Customer waiting times
D   Staff turnover   **(2 marks)**

24.10 Division A of Aigburth Co is considering a project which will increase annual net profit after tax by $30,000 but will require average inventory levels to increase by $200,000. The current target rate of return on investments is 13% and the imputed interest cost of capital is 12%.

Based on the ROI and/or RI criteria would the project be accepted?

A   ROI – yes, RI - no
B   ROI – yes RI - yes
C   ROI – no, RI - yes
D   ROI – no, RI - no   **(2 marks)**

24.11 Which of the following statements are valid criticisms of return on investment (ROI) as a performance measure?

1   It is misleading if used to compare departments with different levels of risk
2   It is misleading if used to compare departments with assets of different ages
3   Its use may discourage investment in new or replacement assets
4   The figures needed are not easily available

A   2 and 3 only
B   2 and 4 only
C   1 and 3 only
D   1, 2 and 3   **(2 marks)**

24.12 Which of the following performance measures would be helpful for a service industry company?

1   Net profit margins
2   Standard costs and variance analysis
3   Employee absentee rates
4   Number of defective units

A   2 and 3 only
B   2 and 4 only
C   1 and 3 only
D   1, 2 and 3   **(2 marks)**

24.13 Which of the following would be suitable for measuring resource utilisation?

1   Efficiency
2   Productivity
3   Relative market share

A   1 and 2 only
B   2 and 3 only
C   1 and 3 only
D   1, 2 and 3   **(2 marks)**

24.14 Which of the following would be suitable for measuring resource utilisation in a parcel delivery company?

A   Number of customer complaints
B   Cost per consignment
C   Depot profit league tables
D   Client evaluation interview   **(2 marks)**

(Total = 28 marks)

25 Cost management   5 mins

25.1 A means of raising the production efficiency of an operating unit by the reorganisation of work is known as:

    A   Work measurement
    B   Work study
    C   Method study
    D   Method measurement   **(2 marks)**

25.2 Value analysis can achieve which of the following?

    1   Eliminate costs
    2   Reduce costs
    3   Increase quantity sold
    4   Increase sales price

    A   2 and 3 only
    B   1 and 2 only
    C   3 and 4 only
    D   1, 2, 3 and 4   **(2 marks)**

(Total = 4 marks)

26 Mixed Bank 1   48 mins

26.1 The following data relate to Product D.

Material cost per unit	$20.00
Labour cost per unit	$69.40
Production overhead cost per machine hour	$12.58
Machine hours per unit	14
General overhead absorption rate	8% of total production cost

What is the total cost per unit of Product D, to the nearest $0.01?

A $176.12
B $265.52
C $286.76
D $300.12   **(2 marks)**

26.2 A product is made in two consecutive processes. Data for the latest period are as follows:

	Process 1	Process 2
Input (kg)	47,000	42,000
Normal loss (% of input)	8	5
Output (kg)	42,000	38,915

No work in progress is held at any time in either process.

The abnormal loss or abnormal gain arising in each process during the period was:

	Process 1	Process 2
A	Abnormal loss	Abnormal loss
B	Abnormal loss	Abnormal gain
C	Abnormal gain	Abnormal loss
D	Abnormal gain	Abnormal gain

(2 marks)

26.3 The following information is available for a company in the latest period.

	Original budget	Flexed budget	Actual results
Sales and production (units)	11,200	9,500	9,500
	$'000	$'000	$'000
Sales revenue	224.0	190.0	209.0
Direct material	56.0	47.5	57.0
Direct labour	66.0	57.5	56.1
Overhead	27.4	24.0	28.0
Profit	74.6	61.0	67.9

Which of the following statements is correct?

A   Budgeted production volumes were achieved during the period.
B   Direct labour is a variable cost
C   The actual selling price per unit exceeded the standard selling price per unit
D   Direct material cost savings were achieved against the budget cost allowance. **(2 marks)**

26.4 Variable costs are conventionally deemed to

A   be constant per unit of output
B   vary per unit of output as production volume changes
C   be constant in total when production volume changes
D   vary, in total, from period to period when production is constant   **(2 marks)**

26.5 Which of the following criticisms of standard costing apply in all circumstances?

(i) Standard costing can only be used where all operations are repetitive and output is homogeneous.

(ii) Standard costing systems cannot be used in environments which are prone to change. They assume stable conditions.

(iii) Standard costing systems assume that performance to standard is acceptable. They do not encourage continuous improvement.

A Criticism (i)
B Criticism (ii)
C Criticism (iii)
D None of them   **(2 marks)**

26.6 Which of the following relates to capital expenditure?

A Cost of acquiring or enhancing non-current assets
B Expenditure on the manufacture of goods or the provision of services
C Recorded as an asset in the income statement
D Recorded as a liability in the statement of financial position   **(2 marks)**

26.7 Overheads in a factory are apportioned to four production cost centres (A, B, C and D). Direct labour hours are used to absorb overheads in A and B and machine hours are used in C and D. The following information is available:

	Production cost centre			
	A	*B*	*C*	*D*
Overhead expenditure ($)	18,757	29,025	46,340	42,293
Direct labour hours	3,080	6,750	3,760	2,420
Machine hours	580	1,310	3,380	2,640

Which cost centre has the highest hourly overhead absorption rate?

A Production Cost Centre A
B Production Cost Centre B
C Production Cost Centre C
D Production Cost Centre D   **(2 marks)**

26.8 A company sold 56,000 units of its single product in a period for a total revenue of $700,000. Finished inventory increased by 4,000 units in the period. Costs in the period were:

Variable production	$3.60 per unit
Fixed production	$258,000 (absorbed on the actual number of units produced)
Fixed non-production	$144,000

Using absorption costing, what was the profit for the period?

A $82,000
B $96,400
C $113,600
D $123,200   **(2 marks)**

26.9 A company with a single product sells more units than it manufactures in a period.

Which of the following correctly describes the use of marginal costing in comparison with absorption costing in the above situation?

A Both profit and inventory values will be higher
B Both profit and inventory values will be lower
C Profit will be higher; inventory values will be lower
D Profit will be lower; inventory values will be higher   **(2 marks)**

26.10 What is a by-product?

A   A product produced at the same time as other products which has no value

B   A product produced at the same time as other products which requires further processing to put it in a saleable state

C   A product produced at the same time as other products which has a relatively low volume compared with the other products

D   A product produced at the same time as other products which has a relatively low value compared with the other products

(2 marks)

26.11 A company manufactures and sells four types of component. The labour hours available for manufacture are restricted but any quantities of the components can be brought-in from an outside supplier in order to satisfy sales demand. The following further information is provided:

	Component			
	A	B	C	D
	per unit	per unit	per unit	per unit
Selling price ($)	12.00	15.00	18.00	20.00
Variable manufacturing costs ($)	6.00	8.0	9.00	11.50
Bought-in price ($)	11.00	11.50	13.00	16.00
Labour (hours)	0.8	0.8	0.8	0.8

Which is the best component to buy-in in order to maximise profit?

A   Component A
B   Component B
C   Component C
D   Component D

(2 marks)

26.12 An investment project has net present values as follows:

At a discount rate of 5%	$69,700 positive
At a discount rate of 14%	$16,000 positive
At a discount rate of 20%	$10,500 negative

Using the above figures, what is the BEST approximation of the internal rate of return of the investment project?

A   17.6%
B   17.9%
C   18.0%
D   22.7%

(2 marks)

26.13 A company has decided to lease a machine. Six annual payments of $8,000 will be made with the first payment on receipt of the machine. Below is an extract from an annuity table:

Year	Annuity factor 10%
1	0.909
2	1.736
3	2.487
4	3.170
5	3.791
6	4.355

What is the present value of the lease payments at an interest rate of 10%?

A $30,328
B $34,840
C $38,328
D $48,000

(2 marks)

26.14 Which of the following would be best described as a short term tactical plan?

    A   Reviewing cost variances and investigate as appropriate
    B   Comparing actual market share to budget
    C   Lowering the selling price by 15%
    D   Monitoring actual sales to budget   **(2 marks)**

26.15 A company made 17,500 units at a total cost of $16 each. Three quarters of the costs were variable and one quarter fixed. 15,000 units were sold at $25 each. There were no opening inventories.

By how much will the profit calculated using absorption costing principles differ from the profit if marginal costing principles had been used?

    A   The absorption costing profit would be $10,000 less
    B   The absorption costing profit would be $10,000 greater
    C   The absorption costing profit would be $30,000 greater
    D   The absorption costing profit would be $40,000 greater   **(2 marks)**

26.16 A company uses the Economic Order Quantity (EOQ) model to establish reorder quantities. The following information relates to the forthcoming period:

Order costs   = $25 per order

Holding costs   = 105 of purchase price = $4/unit

Annual demand   = 20,000 units

Purchase price   = $40 per unit

EOQ   = 500 units

No safety inventory are held

What are the total annual costs of inventory (ie the total purchase cost plus total order cost plus total holding costs)?

    A $22,000
    B $33,500
    C $802,000
    D $803,000   **(2 marks)**

26.17 If $\Sigma X = 100$, $\Sigma Y = 400$, $\Sigma X^2 = 2,040$, $\Sigma Y^2 = 32,278$, $\Sigma XY = 8,104$ and $n = 5$ which of the following values for a and b are correct in the formula $Y = a + bX$?

	a	b
A	28	−2.6
B	28	+2.6
C	−28	−2.6
D	−28	+2.6

                                                               (2 marks)

26.18 A company is considering accepting a one-year contract which will require four skilled employees. The four skilled employees could be recruited on a one-year contract at a cost of $40,000 per employee. The employees would be supervised by an existing manager who earns $60,000 per annum. It is expected that supervision of the contract would take 10% of the manager's time.

Instead of recruiting new employees the company could retrain some existing employees who currently earn $30,000 per year. The training would cost $15,000 in total. If these employees were used they would need to be replaced at a total cost of $100,000.

The relevant labour cost of the contract is

A $115,000
B $135,000
C $160,000
D $275,000   **(2 marks)**

26.19 For a set of six data pairs for the variable x (profit) and y (sales) the following values have been found.

$\Sigma x = 2$
$\Sigma y = 15$
$\Sigma x^2 = 30$
$\Sigma y^2 = 130$
$\Sigma xy = 14$

The correlation coefficient is:

A   0.0006 (to 4 dp)
B   0.02 (to 2 dp)
C   0.17 (to 2 dp)
D   1.9973 (to 4 dp)   **(2 marks)**

26.20 A company wants to calculate the total cost of a job. The estimated cost for the job is as follows.

Direct materials   10 kg @ $10 per kg
Direct labour   20 hours @ $5 per hour

Variable production overheads are recovered at the rate of $2 per labour hour.

Fixed production overheads for the company are budgeted to be $100,000 each year and are recovered on the basis of labour hours. There are 10,000 budgeted labour hours each year.

Other costs in relation to selling, distribution and administration are recovered at the rate of $50 per job.

The total cost of the job is

A   200
B   400
C   440
D   490   **(2 marks)**

                                                        (Total = 40 marks)

27 Mixed Bank 2   48 mins

27.1   A division of a service company is aware that its recent poor performance has been attributable to a low
       standard of efficiency amongst the workforce, compared to rival firms. The company is adopting a
       balanced scorecard approach to setting performance targets. As part of its objective of closing the skills
       gap between itself and rival companies, the division's management has set a target of providing at least
       40 hours of training each year for all its employees.

       What does this performance target reflect?

       A   A customer perspective
       B   A learning and growth perspective
       C   An internal process perspective
       D   A finance perspective   **(2 marks)**

27.2   Which of the following could be included in a time series based sales forecast?

       1   Trend
       2   Seasonal variation
       3   Cyclical variation
       4   Random fluctuation

       A   1 only
       B   2 only
       C   1, 2 and 3 only
       D   1, 2, 3 and 4   **(2 marks)**

27.3   Which of the following is the best definition of return on capital employed?

       A   Profit before interest and tax ÷ Ordinary shareholders' funds × 100
       B   Profit before interest and tax ÷ (Ordinary shareholders' funds + Non-current liabilities) × 100
       C   Profit after interest and tax ÷ Ordinary shareholders' funds × 100
       D   Profit after interest and tax ÷ (Ordinary shareholders' funds + Non-current liabilities) × 100
                                                                             (2 marks)

27.4   A company uses total quality management (TQM) and has recorded the following costs of quality for a period.

       Staff training $8,000
       Inspection $12,000
       Warranty claims $20,000
       Rework of faulty items detected before delivery to customers $15,000

             What would be the net benefit of spending an extra

       A $2,000
       B $3,200
       C $5,000
       D $6,200   **(2 marks)**

27.5   Which of the following costs would be considered to be the responsibility of the manager of a profit
       centre?

       1   Direct labour
       2   Variable production overhead
       3   Imputed interest on capital invested
       4   Depreciation on machinery

       A   1 and 2 only
       B   1, 2 and 3 only
       C   1, 2, 3 and 4
       D   3 and 4 only   **(2 marks)**

27.6 In a period 12,250 units were made and there was a favourable labour efficiency variance of $11,250. If 41,000 labour hours were worked and the standard wage rate was $6 per hour, how many standard hours (to two decimal places) were allowed per unit?

A   3.19
B   3.35
C   3.50
D   6.00

(2 marks)

27.7 In its first year of operations a company produced 100,000 units of a produc and sold 80,000 units at $9 per unit. It earned a marginal costing profit of $200,000. It calculates that its fixed production overhead per unit is $5.

What profit would it have earned under an absorption costing system?

A $100,000
B $200,000
C $300,000
D $320,000

(2 marks)

27.8 The table below contains details of an airline's expenditure on aviation fuel.

Year	Total expenditure on aviation fuel $ million	Total distance flown km million	Fuel price index
20X8	600	4,200	120
20X9	1,440	4,620	240

The following statements relate to the changes between 20X8 and 20X9.

1   The quantity of fuel consumed increased by 140%
2   The quantity of fuel consumed increased by 20%
3   The quantity of fuel consumed per km flown increased by 20%
4   The quantity of fuel consumed per km flown increased by 109%

Which statements are true?

A   1 only
B   2 only
C   2 and 3 only
D   2 and 4 only

(2 marks)

27.9 The following statements relate to spreadsheets.

Which statement is false?

A   They are an efficient method of storing text based files
B   They facilitate 'what if' analysis
C   They allow data to be displayed graphically
D   They allow the font, size and colour of text to be changed

(2 marks)

27.10 A company budgeted to sell 5,000 units of a product in November at a standard price of $30 per unit and to earn a profit of $25,000. It actually sold 6,000 units at $28 per unit and earned a profit of $32,000.

What was the favourable sales volume profit variance for November?

A $5,000
B $7,000
C $12,000
D $30,000

(2 marks)

27.11 Which of the following are benefits of using activity based costing?

    1   It recognises that overhead costs are not always driven by the volume of production
    2   It does not result in under or over absorption of foxed overheads
    3   It avoids all arbitrary cost apportionments
    4   It is particularly useful in single product businesses

    A   1 only
    B   1 and 2 only
    C   2 and 3 only
    D   1 and 4 only   **(2 marks)**

27.12 An investment project has net present values as follows.

At a discount rate of 5%	$69,700 positive
At a discount rate of 14%	$16,000 positive
At a discount rate of 20%	$10,500 negative

Using the above figures what is the best approximation of the internal rate of return of the investment project?

    A   17.6%
    B   17.9%
    C   18.0%
    D   22.7%   **(2 marks)**

27.13 A company uses production labour hours to absorb its fixed production overheads. A strike by its workforce results in a loss of 30% of the period's budgeted production labour hours.

Which of the following variances will occur as a result of the loss in production labour hours?

    A   Adverse fixed overhead capacity variance
    B   Adverse fixed overhead efficiency variance
    C   Adverse direct labour efficiency variance
    D   Adverse direct labour rate variance   **(2 marks)**

27.14 A firm with current assets of $40 million and current liabilities of $20 million buys $5 million of inventory on credit which increases its inventory level to $10 million.

What will the effect be on its current ratio and quick (acid test) ratio?

	Current ratio	Liquidity ratio
A	Increase by 25%	Unchanged
B	Reduce by 10%	Unchanged
C	Increase by 25%	Reduce by 20%
D	Reduce by 10%	Reduce by 20%

                                                    (2 marks)

27.15 A publishing company is researching the reading habits of the United Kingdom's population. It randomly selects a number of locations from around the UK and then interviews everyone who lives in these locations.

What is this approach to sampling known as?

    A   Systematic sampling
    B   Stratified sampling
    C   Quota sampling
    D   Cluster sampling   **(2 marks)**

27.16 A company has a single product with a selling price of $12 per unit, which is calculated as variable cost per unit, plus 20%. At an output level of 5,000 units it makes a loss of $8,000

What is the company's total fixed cost?

A $2,000
B $4,000
C $18,000
D $20,000   **(2 marks)**

The following information relates to questions 27.17 and 27.18

The following data are available for product X

	Period Budget	Period Actual
Sales units	5,000	5,200
	$	$
Sales revenue	50,000	57,200
Manufacturing cost	30,000	31,200
Profit	20,000	26,000

      (2 marks)

27.17 What is the sales price variance?

A $5,200 adverse
B $5,000 favourable
C $5,200 favourable
D $7,200 favourable   **(2 marks)**

27.18 What is the sales volume profit variance?

A $800 favourable
B $1,000 favourable
C $6,000 favourable
D $7,200 adverse   **(2 marks)**

27.19 A firm has used linear regression analysis to establish the relationship between total cost and activity in units.

What does the slope of the regression line represent?

A   The variable cost per unit
B   The fixed cost per unit
C   The average cost per unit
D   Total variable costs   **(2 marks)**

27.20 A division has a capital employed of $2,000,000 and earns an operating profit of $600,000. It is considering a project that will increase operating profit by $20,000 but would increase its capital employed by $80,000. A rate of 15% is used to compute interest on capital employed.

What will be the effect on residual income and return on capital employed if the division accepts the project?

	Residual income	Return on investment
A	Increase	Increase
B	Increase	Decrease
C	Decrease	Increase
D	Decrease	Decrease

      (2 marks)

      (Total = 40 marks)

Answers

1 Accounting for management

1.1   C   Complete accuracy is not necessarily an **essential** quality of good information. It needs to be **sufficiently accurate** for its purpose, and often there is no need to go into unnecessary detail for pointless accuracy.

1.2   B   Tactical planning is used by middle management to decide how the resources of the business should be employed to achieve specific objectives in the most efficient and effective way.

1.3   D   Management accounts often incorporate non-monetary measures. Therefore **statement 1** is incorrect.

              There is no legal requirement to prepare management accounts. Therefore **statement 2** is incorrect.

              Management accounts do serve as a future planning tool, but they are also useful as an historical record of performance. Therefore **statement 3** is incorrect.

1.4   D   **Statement 1** is a description of a management information system, not a management control system.

              Statement 2 is the 'wrong way round'. The strategy is the course of action that a business might pursue in order to achieve its objectives.

              Statement 3 is correct. Data is the 'raw material' which is processed into useful information.

1.5   B   Good information is not necessarily extensive. Too much information may tend to obscure the important points.

1.6   A   Monthly variance reports are an example of tactical management information.

1.7   B   1 is false. **Strategic planning** is carried out by senior management. Front line managers will be concerned with **operational planning**. 2 is true. The management accountant may frequently have to take into account non-financial information

2 Sources of data

2.1   D   Data collected by survey for a particular project are a primary data source.

              Historical records of transport costs were not collected specifically for the preparation of forecasts, therefore these are secondary data.

              The *Annual Abstract of Statistics* is a source of secondary external data.

2.2   D   It is primary data that is collected for a specific purpose so (i) is false. Continuous data can take on any value so (ii) is false. Both (iii) and (iv) are true.

2.3   C   A **sampling frame** is a numbered list of all items in a **population** (not a **sample**).

              Cluster sampling involves selecting one definable subsection of the population which therefore makes the potential for bias considerable.

2.4   C   The only sampling method that does not require a sampling frame is quota sampling, therefore C is the correct option.

2.5   D   In quota sampling, investigators are told to interview all of the people they meet up to a certain quota.

3 Cost classification

3.1 B The royalty cost can be traced in full to the product, ie it has been incurred as a direct consequence of making the product. It is therefore a direct expense. **Options A, C and D** are all overheads or indirect costs which cannot be traced directly and in full to the product.

3.2 B The wages paid to the stores assistant cannot be traced in full to a product or service, therefore this is an indirect labour cost.

3.3 B Overtime premium is always classed as factory overheads unless it is:

- Worked at the specific request of a customer to get his order completed.

- Worked regularly by a production department in the normal course of operations, in which case it is usually incorporated into the direct labour hourly rate.

3.4 D Indirect costs are those which **cannot be easily identified** with a specific cost unit. Although the staples could probably be identified with a specific chair, the cost is likely to be relatively insignificant. The expense of tracing such costs does not usually justify the possible benefits from calculating more accurate direct costs. The cost of the staples would therefore be treated as an indirect cost, to be included as a part of the overhead absorption rate.

3.5 D The manager of a profit centre usually has control over how revenue is raised, ie selling prices (item (i)) and over the controllable costs incurred in the centre (item (ii)).

Apportioned head office costs (item (iii)) are uncontrollable from the point of view of the profit centre manager. A responsibility centre manager does not have control over the capital investment in the centre (item (iv)) unless the centre is designated an investment centre.

3.6 C Controllable costs are items of expenditure which can be directly influenced by a given manager within a given time span.

3.7 D It would be appropriate to use the cost per customer account and the cost per cheque received and processed for control purposes. Therefore **items (ii) and (iii)** are suitable cost units.

Stationery costs, **item (i)**, is an expense of the department, therefore it is not a suitable cost unit.

3.8 A A period cost is charged against the sales for the period. It is not carried forward in inventory to a future period.

3.9 C The supervisors are engaged in the production activity, therefore **option D** can be eliminated. They supervise the production of all products, therefore their salaries are indirect costs because they cannot be specifically identified with a cost unit. This eliminates **options A and B**. The salaries are indirect production overhead costs, therefore **option C** is correct.

3.10 A Remember you are only looking for costs that are **directly related** to getting the finished goods from the production line to your customers. Before they can be distributed, finished goods may have to be temporarily **stored** in a warehouse therefore the **rental** of the warehouse will be regarded as a **distribution cost**. In addition, you will need **delivery vehicles** for distribution purposes – any costs related to these vehicles will be classed as distribution costs. Hence both **(i) and (ii)** are distribution costs **(option A)**. Commission paid to sales staff is a **selling cost**.

3.11 B A function or location for which costs are ascertained. A cost centre acts as a 'collecting place' for costs before they are analysed further.

4 Cost behaviour

4.1   B   Within the relevant range, fixed costs are not affected by the level of activity, therefore **option B** is correct.

4.2   B   Variable overhead $= \dfrac{97,850 - 84,865}{15,950 - 13,500} = \dfrac{12,985}{2,450}$

$\qquad\qquad\qquad\qquad\qquad\quad = \$5.30$ per square metre

Fixed overhead $= 84,865 - (\$5.30 \times 13,500)$
$\qquad\qquad\qquad\qquad = \$84,865 - \$71,550 = \$13,315$

Overheads on 18,300 square metres $= \$13,315 + (5.30 \times 18,300)$
$\qquad\qquad\qquad\qquad\qquad\qquad\qquad\quad = \$13,315 + \$96,990$
$\qquad\qquad\qquad\qquad\qquad\qquad\qquad\quad = \$110,305$

4.3   B   Graph 2 shows that costs increase in line with activity levels

4.4   A   Graph 1 shows that fixed costs remain the same whatever the level of activity

4.5   A   Graph 1 shows that cost per unit remains the same at different levels of activity

4.6   C   Graph 4 shows that semi-variable costs have a fixed element and a variable element

4.7   A   Graph 3 shows that the step fixed costs go up in 'steps' as the level of activity increases

4.8   C

	Units	$
High output	1,100	18,300
Low output	700	13,500
Variable cost of	400	4,800

Variable cost per unit $4,800/$400 = $12 per unit

Fixed costs = $18,300 − ($12 × 1,100) = $5,100

Therefore the correct answer is C.

4.9   D   The salary is part fixed ($650 per month) and part variable (5 pence per unit). Therefore it is a semi-variable cost and answer D is correct.

4.10   D   The cost described will increase in **steps**, remaining fixed at each step until another supervisor is required. Such a cost is known as a **step cost**.

4.11   A   Independent Variable x = advertising expenditure

Dependent variable y = sales revenue

Highest x = month 6 = $6,500
Highest y = month 6 = $225,000

Lowest x = month 2 = $2,500
Lowest y = month 2 = $125,000
Using the high-low method:

	Advertising expenditure $	Sales revenue $
Highest	6,500	225,000
Lowest	2,500	125,000
	4,000	100,000

Sales revenue generated for every $1 spent on advertising $= \dfrac{\$100,000}{\$4,000} = \$25$ per $1 spent.

∴ If $6,500 is spent on advertising, expected sales revenue = $6,500 × $25 = $162,500

∴ Sales revenue expected without any expenditure on advertising = $225,000 − $162,500 = $62,500

∴ Sales revenue = 62,500 = (25 × advertising expenditure)

4.12   D   The cost described is a stepped fixed cost. A stepped fixed cost is fixed in nature but only within
           certain levels of activity.

4.13   B

	Activity level $	Cost $
Highest	10,000	400,000
Lowest	5,000	250,000
	5,000	150,000

Variable cost per unit $= \dfrac{\$150,000}{5,000\,units} = \$30$

4.14   A   The diagram shown depicts annual factory power cost where the electricity supplier sets a tariff
           based on a fixed charge plus a constant unit cost for consumption but subject to maximising
           arrival charge.

4.15   C   Using the high-low method:

	Units	Cost $
	20,000	40,000
	4,000	20,000
	16,000	20,000

Variable cost per unit $= \dfrac{\$20,000}{16,000\,units}$

$= \$1.25$

4.16   A   Graph A shows that up to 30,000 units, each unit costs a constant price per unit. After 30,000
           units, the gradient of the new variable cost line is more gentle which indicates that the cost per
           unit is lower than the cost when 0 – 30,000 units are purchased.

4.17   C

	Production Units	Total cost $
Level 2	5,000	9,250
Level 1	3,000	6,750
	2,000	2,500

Variable cost per unit $= \dfrac{\$2,500}{2,000\,units}$

$= \$1.25$ per unit

Fixed overhead $= \$9,250 - (\$1.25 \times 5,000) = \$3,000$

4.18   B   The variable cost per X-ray is $15.50

	X-rays No	Overheads $
	4,750	273,625
	4,500	269,750
Variable cost of	250	3,875

Variable cost per X-ray $= \$3,875/250 = \$15.50$

4.19   D   The delivery costs for a sales volume of 700 units will be $ ⌐11,500⌐

Using the high-low method

	Units	Total costs $
High	800	12,000
Low	400	10,000
	400	2,000

$$\text{Variable cost per unit} = \frac{\$2,000}{400} = \$5$$

Total costs = fixed costs + variable costs
Let x = fixed costs
$12,000   = x + (800 × $5)
$12,000   = x + $4,000
x   = $12,000 – $4,000
       = $8,000
For a sales volume of 700 units
Total costs = fixed costs + variable costs
= $8,000 + (700 × $5)
= $8,000 + $3,500 = $11,500

5 Presenting information

5.1	C	Material	Cost $	Percentage %	Degrees
		W	2,250	25	90
		X	3,000	33.3	120
		Y	3,600	40	144
		Z	150	1.7	6
			9,000	100	360

3,600/9,000 × 360° = 144°

5.2   B   Multiple bar chart

5.3   C   After May, sales of strawberry began to catch up with sales of chocolate.

6 Material costs

6.1   A   Among other things, the GRN is used to update the inventory records and to check that the quantity invoiced by the supplier was actually received. The GRN does not usually contain price information. Therefore the correct answer is A.

6.2   A   Free inventory balance = units in inventory + units on order from suppliers – units outstanding on customers' orders

13,000   = units in inventory + 27,500 – 16,250

∴ Units in inventory = 13,000 – 27,500 + 16,250 = 1,750

6.3   C   Reorder level = maximum usage × maximum lead time
= 95 × 18
= 1,710 units

6.4   C   Maximum level = reorder level + reorder quantity – (minimum usage × minimum lead time)
= 1,710 + 1,750 – (50 × 12) = 2,860 units

6.5   C $EOQ = \sqrt{\dfrac{2CoD}{C_h}} = \dfrac{2 \times \$80 \times 2,500}{\$15} = 163$

6.6   D   Stock-outs arise when too little inventory is held (i); safety inventories are the level of units maintained in case there is unexpected demand (ii); and a reorder level can be established by looking at the maximum usage and the maximum lead-time (iii). Therefore, they are all correct statements with regards to inventories.

6.7   C   The economic batch quantity is used to establish the cumulative production quantity.

6.8   D $$EOQ = \sqrt{\frac{2C_oD}{C_H}}$$

Where C_o = 20
D   = 12,500 × 4 = 50,000
C_H = 10% × $15 = 1.50

$$EOQ = \sqrt{\frac{2 \times 20 \times 50,000}{1.50}}$$

$$= \sqrt{1,333,333}$$

$$= 1,155 \text{ units}$$

6.9   D   If there is a decrease in the cost of ordering a batch of raw material, then the EOQ will also be lower (as the numerator in the EOQ equation will be lower). If the EOQ is lower, than average inventory held (EOQ/2) with also be lower and therefore the total annual holding costs will also be lower.

6.10   C   Reorder level = maximum usage × maximum lead time
                      = 520 × 15
                      = 7,800 units

6.11   C   Statement (i) is not correct. A debit to stores with a corresponding credit to work in progress (WIP) indicates that **direct materials returned** from production were $18,000.

Statement (ii) is correct. **Direct costs of production** are 'collected' in the WIP account.

Statement (iii) is correct. **Indirect costs of production or overhead** are 'collected' in the overhead control account.

Statement (iv) is correct. The purchases of materials on credit are credited to the creditors account and debited to the material stores control account.

Therefore the correct answer is C.

6.12   C   Annual holding cost

= [buffer (safety) inventory + reorder level/2)] x holding cost per unit

= [500 + (2,000/2)] x $2

= $3,000

6.13   D   The economic order quantity is 300 units.

The formula for the economic order quantity (EOQ) is

$$EOQ = \sqrt{\frac{2C_oD}{C_h}}$$

With C_o = $10

D   = 5,400 ÷ 12 = 450 per month

C_h = $0.10

$$EOQ = \sqrt{\frac{2 \times \$10 \times 450}{\$0.10}}$$

$$= \sqrt{90,000}$$

$$= 300 \text{ units}$$

6.14   A   The level of safety inventory is ⌐400⌐ units (to the nearest whole unit).

Let x = safety inventory

Average inventory = safety inventory (x) + $\dfrac{\text{reorder quantity}}{2}$

3,400	=	$x + \dfrac{6,000}{2}$
3,400	=	x + 3,000
x	=	3,400 – 3,000
∴ x	=	<u>400 units</u>

6.15   A   The economic order quantity is 175 units (to the nearest whole unit).

$$EOQ = \sqrt{\frac{2C_0 D}{C_h}}$$

$$= \sqrt{\frac{2 \times \$100 \times 1,225}{\$8}}$$

$$= \sqrt{30,625}$$

= 175 units

6.16   B   The maximum inventory level was 6,180 units

Reorder level	= maximum usage × maximum lead time
	= 130 × 26 = 3,380 units
Maximum level	= reorder level + reorder quantity – (minimum usage × minimum lead time)
	= 3,380 + 4,000 – (60 × 20)
	= 6,180 units

6.17   C

$$EBQ = \sqrt{\frac{2C_0 D}{C_h(1 - D/R)}}$$

$$Q = \sqrt{\frac{2 \times 125 \times 5,000}{0.0025(1 - 5,000/10,000)}}$$

$$= \sqrt{\frac{1,250,000}{0.00125}}$$

= 31,623 units

7   Accounting for labour

7.1   D   Budgeted hours = 3,000 + 8,000 + 7,000 + 9,000 = 27,000

Capacity ratio = $\dfrac{\text{actual hours worked}}{\text{budgeted hours}} = \dfrac{29,000}{27,000} \times 100\% = 107.4\%$

7.2   A

Product	Units	Standard hours	
W	12,000	(× 0.2)	2,400
X	25,000	(× 0.4)	10,000
Y	16,000	(× 0.5)	8,000
Z	5,000	(× 1.5)	7,500
			27,900

$$\text{Efficiency ratio} = \frac{\text{Standard hours produced}}{\text{Actual hours worked}} = \frac{27,900}{29,000} \times 100\% = 96.2\%$$

7.3 A The graph shows a constant wage up to a certain level of output, which is payable even at zero output. This is the minimum guaranteed wage. Above a certain output the wage cost rises at a constant rate. This is the piece rate payable in addition to the minimum wage.

Graphs for the other options would look like this:

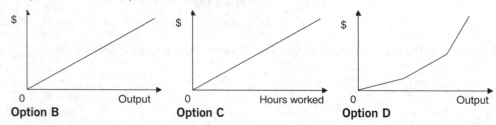

Option B   **Option C**   **Option D**

7.4 B

	Hours
Standard time for 180 units ($\times$ 4/60)	12
Actual time taken	7
Time saved	5

	$
Basic pay 7 hours $\times$ $5	35
Bonus: 60% $\times$ 5 hours saved $\times$ $5 per hour	15
	50

7.5 A Number of units qualifying for payment $= 210 - 17$
                                                                                  $= 193$

Piecework payment to be made:

	$
First 100 units @ $0.20	20.00
Last 93 units @ $0.30	27.90
	47.90

7.6 C The overtime premium paid at the specific request of a customer would be treated as a direct cost because it can be traced to a specific cost unit.

The four hours of machine breakdown is idle time. It cannot be traced to a specific cost unit therefore it is an indirect cost.

The direct wages cost is as follows.

	$
Basic pay for active hours (38 hours $\times$ $3.60)	136.80
Overtime premium re: customer request (2 hours $\times$ $1.80)	3.60
	140.40

7.7 C Group bonus schemes are useful to reward performance when production is integrated so that all members of the group must work harder to increase output, for example in production line manufacture. **Statement (i)** is therefore true.

Group bonus schemes are not effective in linking the reward to a particular individual's performance. Even if one individual makes a supreme effort, this can be negated by poor performance from other members of the group. Therefore **statement (ii)** is not true.

Non-production employees can be included in a group incentive scheme, for example when all employees in a management accounting department must work harder to produce prompt budgetary control reports. **Statement (iii)** is therefore true, and the correct option is C.

7.8 B The overtime was not worked for any specific job and is therefore an **indirect wages cost** to be 'collected' in the overhead control account. Similarly, the holiday pay is an **indirect cost**, therefore the total **debit to the overhead control account** is $2,500. The **direct wages** of $70,800 is

debited to the work in progress account and the total wages cost is **credited to the wages control account**.

7.9   B   Reduction in number of employees   = 30 – 20 = 10
          Number of employees leaving   = 15
          ∴ Number of employees replaced   = 15 – 10 = 5

$$\text{Labour turnover rate} = \frac{\text{replacements}}{\text{average no. of employees in period}} \times 100\%$$

$$= \frac{5}{(30 + 20) \div 2} \times 100\%$$

$$= 20\%$$

7.10 A

	Hours
Standard time for 80 units (× 9/60)	12
Actual time taken	8
Time saved	4

Group bonus : 70% × 4 hours saved × $6 per hour = $16.80

Jane's share of bonus = 50% × ($16.80 × 60%)
                      = $5.04

7.11 C   DR   Overhead control   CR   Wages control

Indirect wages are 'collected' in the overhead control account, for subsequent absorption into work in progress.

8   Accounting for overheads

8.1   D   Number of employees in packing department = 2 direct + 1 indirect = 3

Number of employees in all production departments = 15 direct + 6 indirect = 21

Packing department overhead

Canteen cost apportioned to packing department	=	$\dfrac{\$8,400}{21} \times 3$
	=	$1,200
Original overhead allocated and apportioned	=	$8,960
Total overhead after apportionment of canteen costs	=	$10,160

8.2   D   Department 1 appears to undertake primarily machine-based work, therefore a machine-hour rate would be most appropriate.

$$\frac{\$27,000}{45,000} = \$0.60 \text{ per machine hour}$$

Therefore the correct answer is D.

8.3   C   Department 2 appears to be labour-intensive therefore a direct labour-hour rate would be most appropriate.

$$\frac{\$18,000}{25,000} = \$0.72 \text{ per direct labour hour}$$

8.4   A   **Statement (i)** is correct because a constant unit absorption rate is used throughout the period.
          Statement (ii) is correct because 'actual' overhead costs, based on actual overhead expenditure and actual activity for the period, cannot be determined until after the end of the period.
          Statement (iii) is incorrect because under/over absorption of overheads is caused by the use of predetermined overhead absorption rates.

8.5 A **Description B** could lead to under-absorbed overheads if actual overheads far exceeded both budgeted overheads and the overhead absorbed. **Description C** could lead to under-absorbed overheads if overhead absorbed does not increase in line with actual overhead incurred.

8.6 B Budgeted absorption rate for fixed overhead   = $360,000/8,000

$\qquad\qquad\qquad\qquad\qquad\qquad\qquad\qquad\qquad\quad$ = $45 per unit

Fixed overhead absorbed = 9,000 units × $45

$\qquad\qquad\qquad\qquad\qquad\qquad$ = $405,000

8.7 A

Actual fixed overhead incurred	$432,000
=	
Fixed overhead absorbed =	$405,000 (from question 6)
Fixed overhead under absorbed	$27,000

8.8 C The insurance cost is likely to be linked to the cost of replacing the machines, therefore the most appropriate basis for apportionment is the value of machinery.

8.9 A All of the overhead absorption methods are suitable, depending on the circumstances.

Method 1, direct labour hours, is suitable in a labour-intensive environment.

Method 2, machine hours, is suitable in a machine-intensive environment.

Method 3, a percentage of prime costs, can be used if it is difficult to obtain the necessary information to use a time-based method. **Method 4**, a rate per unit, is suitable if all cost units are identical.

8.10 C Statement (i) is correct. The cost of indirect material issued is 'collected' in the overhead control account **pending absorption into work in progress**.

Statement (ii) is incorrect. The overhead cost **incurred** was $210,000. The overhead **absorbed into work in progress** during the period was $404,800.

Statement (iii) is incorrect. The $8,400 is **debited to profit and loss**, indicating an extra charge to compensate for the overhead **under absorbed.**

Statement (iv) is correct. The indirect wage cost is 'collected' in the overhead control account **pending absorption into work in progress**.

Therefore the correct answer is C.

8.11 A Only production related costs should be considered when considering the allocation, apportionment and reapportionment of overhead in an absorption costing situation.

8.12 A

	$
Actual fixed production overheads	×
Absorbed fixed production overheads (4,500 × $8)	36,000
Over-absorbed fixed production overheads	6,000

Actual fixed production overheads = $36,000 – $6,000

$\qquad\qquad\qquad\qquad\qquad\qquad\qquad\quad$ = $30,000

8.13 D

	Production cost centre	
	Primary	Finishing
Allocated and apportioned	$96,000	$82,500
Total direct labour hours	9,600 hours	6,875 hours
Fixed overhead absorption rate	$10 per hour	$12 per hour

Workings

(W1)

Total direct labour hours – Primary	= (6,000 × 36/60) hours + (7,500 × 48/60) hours
	= (3,600 + 6,000) hours
	= 9,600 hours

(W2)

Total direct labour hours – Finishing	$= (6,000 \times 25/60)$ hours $+ (7,500 \times 35/60)$ hours
	$= (2,500 + 4,375)$ hours
	$= 6,875$ hours

Budgeted fixed overhead cost per unit for Product Y

Primary	$= 48$ minutes/60 minutes $\times$ \$10 per hour
	$= \$8$ per unit
Finishing	$= 35$ minutes/60 minutes $\times$ \$12 per hour
	$= \$7$ per unit
Total	$= \$8 + \$7$
	$= \$15$ per unit of Product Y

8.14 A

	$
Absorbed overhead (30,000 hours $\times$ \$3.50)	105,000
Actual overhead	108,875
Under-absorbed overhead	3,875

8.15 D   Using simultaneous equations:

Let P = overheads for department P after reapportionment
X = overheads for department X after reapportionment
Y = overheads for department Y after reapportionment

$$P = 95,000 + 0.4X + 0.3Y$$
$$X = 46,000 + 0.1Y$$
$$Y = 30,000 + 0.2X$$

$$X = 46,000 + 0.1 (30,000 + 0.2X)$$
$$X = 46,000 + 3,000 + 0.02X$$
$$X = 49,000 + 0.02X$$
$$X - 0.02X = 49,000$$
$$0.98X = 49,000$$
$$X = 49,000/0.98$$
$$= 50,000$$

If X = 50,000
$$Y = 30,000 + (0.2 \times 50,000)$$
$$Y = 30,000 + 10,000$$
$$Y = 40,000$$
$$\therefore X = 50,000 \text{ and } Y = 40,000$$

$$\therefore P = 95,000 + 0.4X + 0.3Y$$
$$= 95,000 + (0.4 \times 50,000 + (0.3 \times 40,000)$$
$$= 95,000 + 20,000 + 12,000$$
$$= 127,000$$

8.16 D

Production overhead absorption rate	$= \$150,000/60,000$
	$= \$2.50$ per machine hour
Production overhead absorbed	$= \$2.50 \times 55,000$ hours
	$= \$137,500$
Production overhead incurred	$= \$150,000$
Production overhead under absorbed	$= \$\ 12,500$

8.17 A   The number of machine hours (to the nearest hour) budgeted to be worked were $\boxed{14,850}$ hours.

$$\text{Budgeted hours} = \frac{\text{Budgeted overheads}}{\text{Budgeted overhead absorption rate}}$$

$$= \frac{\$475,200}{\$32}$$

$$= \underline{14,850}$$

8.18 B   The machine hour absorption rate is (to the nearest $) $45 per machine hour.

$$\text{Machine hour absorption rate} = \frac{\text{Budgeted overheads}}{\text{Budgeted machine hours}}$$

$$= \frac{\$690,480}{15,344}$$

$$= \$45 \text{ per machine hour}$$

8.19 C   The budgeted overhead absorption rate was $25 per machine hour (to the nearest $).

	$
Actual overheads incurred	496,500
Over-absorbed overhead	64,375
Actual overheads absorbed	560,875

$$\frac{\text{Actual overheads absorbed}}{\text{Actual machine hours}} = \text{Amount absorbed per machine hour}$$

$$\frac{\$560,875}{22,435} = \$25 \text{ per machine hour}$$

8.20 D   Fixed production overhead was under absorbed by $25,000

	$
Overhead absorbed (110,000 std hours × $2.50)	275,000
Overhead incurred	300,000
Overhead under absorbed	25,000

The overhead is under absorbed because the overhead absorbed was less than the overhead incurred.

9 Absorption costing and marginal costing

9.1 D   We know that the profit using marginal costing would be higher than the absorption costing profit, because inventories are decreasing. However, we cannot calculate the value of the difference without the fixed overhead absorption rate per unit.

$$\text{Difference in profit} = \frac{2,000 \text{ units inventory}}{\text{reduction}} \times \frac{\text{fixed overhead absorption}}{\text{rate per unit}}$$

9.2 B   Difference in profit = change in inventory level × fixed overhead per unit
= (2,400 – 2,700) × ($4 × 3)
= $3,600

The absorption profit will be higher because inventories have increased, and fixed overheads have been carried forward in inventories.

9.3 A   Difference in profit = change in inventory level × fixed overhead per unit
= (15,000 – 20,000) × $8
= $40,000

The inventory level increased during the period therefore the absorption costing profit is higher than the marginal costing profit.

Marginal costing profit = $130,000 – $40,000 = $90,000

9.4   A   Contribution per unit   = $30 – $(6.00 + 7.50 + 2.50)
                                          = $14

Contribution for month   = $14 × 5,200 units
                                          = $72,800

Less fixed costs incurred   = $27,400

Marginal costing profit   = $45,400

9.5   D

	$	$
Sales (5,200 at $30)		156,000
Materials (5,200 at $6)	31,200	
Labour (5,200 at $7.50)	39,000	
Variable overhead (5,200 at $2.50)	13,000	
Total variable cost		(83,200)
Fixed overhead ($5 × 5,200)		(26,000)
Over-absorbed overhead (W)		1,600
Absorption costing profit		48,400

Working	$
Overhead absorbed (5,800 × $5)	29,000
Overhead incurred	27,400
Over-absorbed overhead	1,600

9.6   B   Inventory levels increased by 3,000 units and absorption costing profit is $105,000 higher ($955,500 – $850,500).

∴ Fixed production cost included in inventory increase:

$$= \frac{\$105,000}{3,000} = \$35 \text{ per unit of inventory}$$

$$\frac{\text{Budgeted fixed costs}}{\text{Fixed cost per unit}} = \frac{\$1,837,500}{£35} = 52,500 \text{ units}$$

9.7   D   Decrease in inventory levels   = 48,500 – 45,500 = 3,000 units

Difference in profits   = $315,250 – $288,250 = $27,000

$$\text{Fixed overhead per unit} \quad = \frac{\$27,000}{3,000} = \$9 \text{ per unit}$$

If you selected one of the other options you attempted various divisions of all the data available in the question!

9.8   C   All of the methods are acceptable bases for absorbing production overheads. However, the **percentage of prime cost has serious limitations** and the rate per unit can only be used if all cost units are identical.

9.9   D   Absorption costing is concerned with including in the total cost of a product an appropriate share of **overhead**, or **indirect cost**. Overheads can be fixed or variable costs, therefore option D is correct. **Option A** and **option B** are incorrect because they relate to direct costs. **Option C** is incorrect because it does not take account of variable overheads.

9.10   C   If inventory levels increase in a period, absorption costing will show a higher profit than marginal costing.

Difference in profit = change in inventory levels × overhead absorption rate per unit

= (750 units – 300 units) × $5 per unit

= 450 units × $5

$= \$2,250$

	$\$$
Marginal costing profit	72,300
Increase in profit	2,250
Absorption costing profit	74,550

9.11 B

Contribution per unit $=$ selling price − variable cost
$= \$10 - \$6$
$= \$4$ per unit

Total contribution $= 250,000$ units $\times \$4$ per unit $= \$1,000,000$
Total fixed costs $= 200,000$ units $\times \$2$ per unit
$= \$400,000$

Marginal costing profit $=$ total contribution − total fixed costs
$= \$1,000,000 - \$400,000$
$= \$600,000$

9.12 D

Breakeven sales revenue $= \dfrac{\text{Fixed costs} + \text{target profit}}{C/S \text{ ratio}}$

$= \dfrac{\$75,000 + \$150,000}{0.75}$

$= \dfrac{\$225,000}{0.75}$

$= \$300,000$

If selling price $= \$10$ per unit

$\dfrac{\$300,000}{\$10} = 30,000$ units must be sold

9.13 C

If inventory levels increase in a period, absorption costing will show a higher profit than marginal costing.

Difference in profit $=$ change in inventory levels $\times$ overhead absorption rate per unit

$= (350 - 100)$ units $\times \$4$ per unit
$= 250$ units $\times \$4$
$= \$1,000$

	$\$$
Marginal costing profit	37,500
Increase in profit	1,000
Absorption costing profit	38,500

9.14 B

Fixed production overhead absorption rate $= \dfrac{\$48,000}{12,000 \text{ units}}$

$= \$4$ per unit

Increase in inventory levels $= (12,000 - 11,720)$ units

$= 280$ units

$\therefore$ Difference in profit $= 280$ units $\times \$4$ per unit

$= \$1,120$

Marginal costing profits are lower than absorption costing profits when stock levels increase in a period, therefore marginal costing profit will be $\$1,120$ lower than absorption costing profits for the same period.

9.15   C   If budgeted fixed overhead expenditure   = 100%

Actual fixed overhead expenditure   = 110%

∴ Variance   = 10%

If variance = \$36,000 = 10% × budgeted fixed overhead expenditure

Budgeted fixed overhead expenditure   = \$36,000/0.1
                                                 = \$360,000

∴ Actual fixed overhead expenditure   = 110% × \$360,000
                                                 = \$396,000

9.16   B   Increase in inventory   = (18,000 – 16,500) units
                                         = 1,500 units

∴ Difference in profit   = 1,500 units × \$10
                                         = \$15,000

Profits under marginal costing will be \$15,000 less than profits under absorption costing ie \$40,000 – \$15,000 = \$25,000.

9.17   D   Any difference between marginal and absorption costing profit is due to changes in inventory.

	\$
Absorption costing profit	2,000
Marginal costing loss	(3,000)
Difference	5,000

Change in inventory   =   Difference in profit/fixed product cost per unit

                        =   \$5,000/\$2 = 2,500 units

Marginal costing loss is lower than absorption costing profit therefore inventory has gone up – that is, production was greater than sales by 2,500 units.

Production = 10,000 units (sales) + 2,500 units = 12,500 units

9.18   D

	Units
Opening inv	900
Closing inv	300
Decrease	600

$$600 \times \left(\frac{\$500,000}{2,500} \right) = 120,000 \text{ lower}$$

10   Job, batch and service costing

10.1   D   **Process costing** is a costing method used where it is not possible to identify separate units of production, or jobs, usually because of the continuous nature of the production process. The manufacture of liquid soap is a **continuous production process.**

10.2   B

	\$
Selling price of job	1,690
Less profit margin (30/130)	390
Total cost of job	1,300
Less overhead	694
Prime cost	606

10.3   A

	$
Direct materials (5 × $20)	100
Direct labour (14 × $8)	112
Variable overhead (14 × $3)	42
Fixed overhead (14 × $5*)	70
Other overhead	80
Total cost of job 173	404

$$\text{*Fixed production overhead absorption rate} = \frac{\$200,000}{40,000}$$
$$= \$5 \text{ per direct labour hour}$$

10.4   C   The most logical basis for absorbing the overhead job costs is to use a percentage of direct labour cost.

$$\begin{aligned}\text{Overhead} &= \frac{\$24,600}{\$(14,500 + 3,500 + 24,600)} \times \$126,000 \\ &= \frac{\$24,600}{\$42,600} \times \$126,000 \\ &= \$72,761 \end{aligned}$$

10.5   C   *Job number*

	WIP $
AA10 (26,800 + 17,275 + 14,500) + ($\frac{14,500}{42,600}$ × 126,000)	101,462
CC20 (18,500 + 24,600 + 72,761)	115,861
	217,323

10.6   C   The actual material and labour costs for a batch **(1 and 4)** can be determined from the material and labour recording system. Actual manufacturing overheads cannot be determined for a specific batch because of the need for allocation and apportionment of each item of overhead expenditure, and the subsequent calculation of a predetermined overhead absorption rate. Therefore **item 2** is incorrect and **item 3** is correct.

10.7   B   Cost per cake would be very small and therefore not an appropriate cost unit. The most appropriate cost unit would be cost per batch.

10.8   B   The vehicle cost per passenger-kilometre (i) is appropriate for cost control purposes because it **combines** the distance travelled and the number of passengers carried, **both of which affect cost**.

The fuel cost for each vehicle per kilometre (ii) can be useful for control purposes because it **focuses on a particular aspect** of the cost of operating each vehicle.

The fixed cost per kilometre (iii) is not particularly useful for control purposes because it **varies with the number of kilometres travelled**.

10.9   B   Number of occupied room-nights = 40 rooms × 30 nights × 65%
= 780

$$\text{Room servicing cost per occupied room-night} = \frac{\$3,900}{780} = \$5$$

10.10 D

Weeks during year	= 52 − 4 = 48
Hours worked per year	= 48 × 35 hours
	= 1,680 hours
Hours chargeable to clients	= 1,680 × 90% = 1,512
Hourly charge rate	= $\frac{\$3,000 + \$18,000}{1,512} = \frac{\$21,000}{1,512}$
	= $13.89 per hour
Price for 3-hour 'colour and cut'	= $13.89 × 3 = $41.67

10.11 A   For most services it is difficult to identify many attributable direct costs. A high level of indirect costs must be shared over several cost units, therefore **option A** is not a characteristic of service costing.

10.12 B   A college and a hotel are likely to use service costing. A plumber works on separately identifiable jobs and is therefore more likely to use job costing.

10.13 C   An airline company, a railway company and a firm of accountants are **all** considered to be service industries.

10.14 C   Assignment 789

	$
Senior consultant – 54 hours × $40	2,160
Junior consultant – 110 hours × $25	2,750
Overhead absorption – 164 hours × $20	3,280
Total cost	8,190
40% × total cost = 40% × $8,190	3,276
Final fee	11,466

10.15 A   Total cost – job number 1012

	$
Direct materials	45
Direct labour	30
Prime cost	75
Production overheads (30/7.5 × $12.50)	50
Total production cost	125
Non-production overheads (0.6 × $75)	45
Total cost – job number 1012	170

11   Process costing

11.1 A   Good production = input – normal loss – abnormal loss
                         = (2,500 – (2,500 × 10%) – 75)kg
                         = 2,500 – 250 – 75
                         = 2,175 kg

11.2 C   Work in progress = 300 litres input – 250 litres to finished goods
                           = 50 litres

Equivalent litres for each cost element are as follows.

	Material		Conversion costs	
	%	Equiv. litres	%	Equiv. litres
50 litres in progress	100	50	50	25

11.3 A   There is no mention of a scrap value available for any losses therefore the normal loss would have a zero value. The normal loss does not carry any of the process costs therefore **options B, C and D** are all incorrect.

11.4 D   Expected output = 2,000 units **less** normal loss (5%) 100 units = 1,900 units

In situation (i) there is an **abnormal loss** of 1,900 – 1,800 = 100 units
In situation (ii) there is an **abnormal gain** of 1,950 – 1,900 = 50 units
In situation (iii) there is an **abnormal gain** of 2,000 – 1,900 = 100 units

Therefore the correct answer is D.

11.5 B   Abnormal losses are valued at the same unit rate as good production, so that their occurrence does not affect the cost of good production.

11.6 D   The total loss was 15% of the material input. The 340 litres of good output therefore represents 85% of the total material input.

Therefore, material input $= \dfrac{340}{0.85} = 400$ litres

11.7 C **Step 1.** **Determine output and losses**

Input	Output	Total	Materials		Labour and overhead	
Units		Units	Units	%	Units	%
	Finished units (balance)	400	400	100	400	100
500	Closing inventory	100	100	100	80	80
500		500	500		480	

Equivalent units

Step 2. **Calculate the cost per equivalent unit**

Input	Cost	Equivalent production in units	Cost per unit
	$		$
Materials	9,000	500	18
Labour and overhead	11,520	480	24
			42

Step 3. **Calculate total cost of output**

Cost of completed units = $42 × 400 units = $16,800

11.8 B Using the data from answer 7 above, extend **step 3** to calculate the value of the work in progress.

Cost element	Number of equivalent units	Cost per equivalent unit	Total
		$	$
Work in progress: Materials	100	18	1,800
Labour & overhead	80	24	1,920
			3,720

11.9 C STATEMENT OF EQUIVALENT UNITS

	Total Units		Materials		Labour		Overheads
Output to process 2*	600		600		600		600
Closing WIP	100	(100%)	100	(50%)	50	(30%)	30
	700		700		650		630

Equivalent units

*500 units input + opening WIP 200 units − closing WIP 100 units.

11.10 B STATEMENT OF COSTS PER EQUIVALENT UNIT

	Materials	Labour	Overheads	Total
	$	$	$	
Opening stock	2,400	1,200	400	
Added during period	6,000	3,350	1,490	
Total cost	8,400	4,550	1,890	
Equivalent units	700	650	630	
Cost per equivalent unit	$12	$7	$3	$22

Value of units transferred to process 2 = 600 units × $22 = $13,200

11.11 D

	Equivalent units				
	Total	*Materials*		*Conversion costs*	
	Units	Units		Units	
Opening inventory	300	300		300	
Fully worked units*	9,550	9,550		9,550	
Output to finished goods	9,850	9,850		9,850	
Closing inventory	450 (100%)	450	(30%)	135	
	10,300	10,300		9,985	

* Fully worked units = input – closing inventory
= (10,000 – 450) units
= 9,550 units

11.12 B Input costs = 2,000 units × $4.50 = $9,000

Conversation costs = $13,340

Normal loss = 5% × 2,000 units × $3 = $300

Expected output = 2,000 units – 100 units = 1,900 units

$$\text{Cost per unit of output} = \frac{\text{Input costs}}{\text{Expected output}}$$

$$= \frac{\$9,000 + \$13,340 - \$300}{1,800\,\text{units}} = \frac{\$22,040}{1,900\,\text{units}} = \$11.6 \text{ (to one decimal point)}$$

11.13 D

	$

Material	9,000
Conversion costs	11,970
Less: scrap value of normal loss (300 × $1.50)	(450)
Cost of process	20,520

Expected output = 3,000 – (10% × 3,000)
= 3,000 – 300 = 2,700 units

$$\text{Costs per unit} = \frac{\text{Input costs } - \text{scrap value of normal loss}}{\text{Expected output}} = \frac{\$20,520}{2,700} = \$7.60$$

Value of output = 2,900 × $7.60 = $22,040

11.14 B Abnormal gain = 276 units – 112 units = 164 units

Cost per unit of good production = $29,744/5,408 = $5.50

∴ Value of abnormal gain = 164 units × $5.50 = $902

The value of the input can be found as the balancing figure in the value columns of the process account.

Polishing process account

	$		$
	---		---
Input (balancing figure)	29,532	Output	29,744
Abnormal gain	902	Normal loss (276 × $2.50)	690
	30,434		30,434

11.15 D Statement (i) is incorrect. Units of normal loss are valued at their scrap value (which may be nil).

Statement (ii) is incorrect. Units of abnormal loss are valued at the same rate as good units.

Therefore the correct answer is D, statements (i) and (ii) both being incorrect.

12 Process costing, joint and by-products

12.1 C   **Total production inventory**

	$
Opening stock	1,000
Direct materials added	10,000
Conversion costs	12,000
	23,000
Less closing inventory	3,000
Total production cost	20,000

	Production		Sales value			Apportioned cost
	Units		$			$
P	4,000	(× $5)	20,000	($20,000 × 20/80)		5,000
R	6,000	(× $10)	60,000	($20,000 × 60/80)		15,000
			80,000			20,000

Product R cost per unit = $15,000/6,000 = $2.50 per unit.

12.2 A   From the previous answer, total production cost to be apportioned = $20,000.

	Production		Apportioned cost
	Units		$
P	4,000	($20,000 × 4/10)	8,000
R	6,000	($20,000 × 6/10)	12,000
	10,000		20,000

12.3 D   **Statement (i)** is incorrect because the value of the product described could be relatively high even though the output volume is relatively low. This product would then be classified as a joint product.

Statement (ii) is incorrect. Since a by-product is not important as a saleable item, it is not separately costed and does not absorb any process costs.

Statement (iii) is correct. These common or joint costs are allocated or apportioned to the joint products.

12.4 B   **Net process costs**

	$
Raw material input	216,000
Conversion costs	72,000
Less by-product revenue	(4,000)
Net process cost	284,000

	Production		Sales value			Apportioned cost
	Units		$			$
E	21,000	(× $15)	315,000	($284,000 × 315/495)		180,727
Q	18,000	(× $10)	180,000	($284,000 × 180/495)		103,273
			495,000			284,000

12.5 C   No costs are apportioned to the by-product. The by-product revenue is credited to the sales account, and so does not affect the process costs.

	Units		Sales value $		Apportioned cost $
L	3,000	(× $32)	96,000	($230,000 × 96/332)	66,506
M	2,000	(× $42)	84,000	($230,000 × 84/332)	58,193
N	4,000	(× $38)	152,000	($230,000 × 152/332)	105,301
			332,000		230,000

12.6 A   Total production units = 412,000 + 228,000

$$= 640,000 \text{ units}$$

Joint costs apportioned to Product H $= \dfrac{228,000}{640,000} \times \$384,000 = \$136,800$

Further processing costs $= \$159,600$

∴ Total product cost of Product H $= \$(136,800 + 159,600) = \$296,400$

∴ Closing inventory value of Product H $= \dfrac{28,000}{228,000} \times \$296,400 = \$36,400$

12.7 D   Sales value of production

W   (12,000 units × $10) $120,000
X   (10,000 units × $12) $120,000

Joint production costs will be apportioned equally between the two products as the sales value of production is the same for each product.

Joint production costs allocated to X = $776,160/2 = $388,080

Value of closing inventory $= \dfrac{2,000}{10,000} \times \$388,080 = \$77,616$

13 Alternative costing principles

13.1 C   ABC is an alternative to traditional volume based methods where production overhead is absorbed on the basis of the volume of direct labour hours or machine hours worked. However, it is still a form of absorption costing because production overheads are absorbed into product costs. ABC identifies costs with support activities and the overhead costs of a product or service could reflect the long-run variable cost of that product or service. ABC can be used for costing services as well as products.

13.2 B   Maturity. During this period, prices tend to fall but profits remain high due to good sales volume.

13.3 B   Life cycle costing looks at costs only but over the product's whole life cycle.

13.4 C   Growth. During the growth phase the product begins to make a profit. This is due to economies of scale being received as increased demand for the product occurs.

13.5 B   Target cost means a product cost estimate derived by subtracting a desired profit margin from a competitive market price.

13.6 A   Growth. The product life cycle stages can be summarised as follows:

Introduction: Basic quality, few competitors, high promotion costs

Growth: As stated in question

Maturity: Most competitive stage, product extension strategies, for example, new markets

Decline: Exit strategy needs to be identified.

14 Forecasting

14.1 C From the data given, it is clear that the correlation is **positive** and **strong**. The correlation coefficient describing a positive strong relationship is 0.98.

14.2 A Y = 20 – 0.25X
X = 12
∴ Y = 20 – 0.25(12) = 17%

14.3 D (i) A correlation coefficient close to +1 or –1 indicates a strong linear relationship between X and Y. The regression equation is therefore more reliable for forecasting.

(ii) Working to a high number of decimal places gives spurious accuracy unless both the data itself is accurate to the same degree and the methods used lend themselves to such precision.

(iii) Forecasting for values of X outside the range of the original data leads to unreliable estimates, because there is no evidence that the same regression relationships hold for such values.

(iv) The regression equation is worthless unless a sufficiently large sample was used to calculate it. In practice, samples of about ten or more are acceptable.

(i) and (iv) increase the reliability of forecasting.

14.4 A The formula for the correlation coefficient is provided in your exam. There are no excuses for getting this question wrong.

$$\text{Correlation coefficient, } r = \frac{n\Sigma XY - \Sigma X\Sigma Y}{\sqrt{[n\Sigma X^2 - (\Sigma X)^2][n\Sigma Y^2 - (\Sigma Y)^2]}}$$

$$= \frac{(4 \times 157) - (12 \times 42)}{\sqrt{[4 \times 46 - 12^2][4 \times 542 - 42^2]}}$$

$$= \frac{628 - 504}{\sqrt{(184 - 144) \times (2,168 - 1,764)}}$$

$$= \frac{124}{\sqrt{40 \times 404}}$$

$$= \frac{124}{127.12}$$

= 0.98 (to 2 decimal places)

14.5 C (i) High levels of correlation do not prove that there is cause and effect.

(ii) A correlation coefficient of 0.73 would generally be regarded as indicating a strong linear relationship between the variables.

(iii) The coefficient of determination provides this information and is given by squaring the correlation coefficient, resulting in 53% in this case.

(iv) The coefficient of determination provides this information and not the correlation coefficient. Remember that you must square the correlation coefficient in order to obtain the coefficient of determination.

Statements (ii) and (iii) are relevant and the correct answer is therefore C.

14.6 D When X = 20, we don't know anything about the relationship between X and Y since the sample data only goes up to X = 10. (i) is therefore true.

Since a correlation coefficient of 0.8 would be regarded as strong (it is a high value) the estimate would be reliable. (ii) is therefore not true.

With such a small sample and the extrapolation required, the estimate is unlikely to be reliable. (iii) is therefore not true.

The sample of only six pairs of values is very small and is therefore likely to reduce the reliability of the estimate. (iv) is therefore true.

The correct answer is therefore D.

14.7 C   The independent variable is denoted by X and the dependent one by Y.

14.8 A $a = \dfrac{\sum y}{n} - b\dfrac{\sum x}{n}$

where b = 17.14

$\sum x$ = 5.75

$\sum y$ = 200

n = 4

$a = \dfrac{200}{4} - 17.14 \times \dfrac{5.75}{4}$

= 50 – (17.14 × 1.4375)
= 50 – 24.64
= 25.36 (to 2 decimal places)

14.9 C $a = \dfrac{\sum y}{n} - b\dfrac{\sum x}{n}$

$= \dfrac{330}{11} - b\dfrac{x440}{11}$

$b = \dfrac{n\sum xy - \sum x \sum y}{n\sum x^2 - (\sum x)^2}$

$= \dfrac{(11 \times 13,467) - (440 \times 330)}{(11 \times 17,986) - 440^2}$

$= \dfrac{148,137 - 145,200}{197,846 - 193,600}$

$= \dfrac{2,937}{4,246}$

= 0.6917

$\therefore a = \dfrac{330}{11} - (0.6917 \times \dfrac{440}{11})$

= 30 – 27.668

= 2.332

= 2.33 (to 2 decimal places)

14.10 C   The correlation coefficient can take on any value from –1 to +1.

14.11 B   y = 7.112 + 3.949x

If x = 19, trend in sales for month 19 = 7.112 + (3.949 × 19) = 82.143

Seasonally-adjusted trend value = 82.143 × 1.12 = 92

If you failed to select the correct option, rework the calculation carefully. You shouldn't have too much trouble with this question since it is just a matter of plugging in a value for x into the equation given in the question.

14.12 A   If $x = 16$, $y = 345.12 - (1.35 \times 16) = 323.52$

            Forecast = trend + seasonal component = $323.52 - 23.62 = 299.9 = 300$ (to nearest unit)

14.13 D $\dfrac{4,700}{0.92} = 5,109$ (to the nearest whole number)

14.14 C $y \quad = 9.82 + (4.372 \times 24)$

            $y \quad = 114.748$

            $\therefore$ forecast $= 114.748 + 8.5$
                             $= 123.248$
                             $= 123$

14.15 B   1   Forecasts are made on the assumption that everything continues as in the past.

            2   If the model being used is inappropriate, for example, if an additive model is used when the trend is changing sharply, forecasts will not be very reliable.

            3   Provided a multiplicative model is used, the fact that the trend is increasing need not have any adverse effect on the reliability of forecasts.

            4   Provided the seasonal variation remains the same in the future as in the past, it will not make forecasts unreliable.

            1 and 2 are therefore necessary and hence the correct answer is B.

14.16 B   Seasonally adjusting the values in a time series removes the seasonal element from the data thereby giving an instant estimate of the trend.

14.17 B $X = 38$ and $Y = 40$

            $\dfrac{X + 36 + Y}{3} = 38$

            $\dfrac{36 + Y + 41}{3} = 39$

            $Y = (3 \times 39) - 36 - 41 = 40$

            $\dfrac{X + 36 + 40}{3} = 38$

            $X = (38 \times 3) - 36 - 40 = 38$

14.18 D   If $t = 1$ in the first quarter of 20X5
                $t = 8$ in the fourth quarter of 20X6

            Trend (Y) $= 65 + (7 \times 8)$
                           $= 121$

            Forecast $=$ trend + seasonal component
                           $= 121 + (-30)$
                           $= 121 - 30$
                           $= 91$

14.19 C   In the first month of 20X9, $t = 13$

            $\therefore$ Y $= \$1,500 - \$(3 \times 13)$
                  $= \$1,461$

            Forecast $=$ trend $\times$ seasonal component
                           $= \$1,461 \times 0.92$
                           $= \$1,344$

14.20 C   1   Provided the multiplicative model is used, it does not matter if the trend is increasing or decreasing.

            2   Forecasts are made on the assumption that the previous trend will continue.

3   In general, extrapolation does not produce reliable estimates but in forecasting the future using time series analysis we have no option but to extrapolate.

4   Forecasts are made on the assumption that previous seasonal variations will continue.

2 and 4 are therefore necessary. The correct answer is C.

14.21 B   When the trend is increasing or decreasing, additive seasonal components change in their importance relative to the trend whereas multiplicative components remain in the same proportion to the trend. Option B is therefore a circumstance in which the multiplicative model would be preferred to the additive model.

14.22 D   Year = 2000

∴ Trend $= (0.0002 \times 2000^2) + (0.4 \times 2000) + 30.4$
$= 800 + 800 + 30.4$
$= 1{,}630.4$

∴ Forecast $= 1.6 \times 1{,}630.4$
$= 2{,}608.64$

∴ Forecast in whole units = 2,609

14.23 B   In 20X9, t = 9

$y = 20t - 10$
$y = (20 \times 9) - 10$
$y = 180 - 10 = 170$

∴ Forecast profits for 20X9 $= 170 - 30 = 140$
$= \$140{,}000$

14.24 D   As this is a multiplicative model, the seasonal variations should sum (in this case) to 4 (an average of 1) as there are four quarters.

Let X = seasonal variation in quarter 4

$1.2 + 1.3 + 0.4 + X = 4$

$2.9 + X = 4$
$X = 4 - 2.9$
$X = 1.1$

14.25 A   For a multiplicative model, the seasonal component S = Y/T
∴T = Y/S

	Quarter	
	1	2
Seasonal component (S)	1.2	1.3
Actual series (Y)	$125,000	$130,000
Trend (T) (= Y/S)	$104,167	$100,000

The trend line for sales has therefore decreased between quarter 1 and quarter 2.

14.26 B   The additive model

$Y = T + S$

where   Y = actual series
T = trend
S = seasonal

The seasonally-adjusted value is an estimate of the trend.

∴ $Y = T + S$
$T = Y - S$
$T = 567{,}800 - (+90{,}100)$
$T = 477{,}700$

14.27 C A Paasche index requires quantities to be ascertained each year and so constructing a Paasche index may therefore be costly. A Laspeyre index only requires them for the base year so (i) is true. The denominator of a Laspeyre index is fixed and therefore the Laspeyre index numbers for several different years can be directly compared. (ii) is therefore false.

14.28 C

$$\text{Fisher's ideal index} = \sqrt{(\text{Laspeyre index} \times \text{Paasche index})}$$

$$= \sqrt{(150.00 \times 138.24)}$$

$$= \sqrt{20,736}$$

$$= 144$$

14.29 C $106 - 91 = 15$

Therefore the price of a bag of cement has gone up 15%.

Therefore price in 20X6 $= 1.15 \times \$0.80$
$= \$0.92$

14.30 C $14.33 (\$5 \times 430 \div 150)$

14.31 C $10 \times 510 \div 130 = \$39.23$

15 Budgeting

15.1 B **Coordination** (i) is an objective of budgeting. Budgets help to ensure that the **activities of all parts of the organisation are coordinated towards a single plan.**

Communication (ii) is an objective of budgeting. The budgetary planning process **communicates targets** to the managers responsible for achieving them, and it should also provide a **mechanism for junior managers to communicate to more senior staff** their estimates of what may be achievable in their part of the business.

Expansion (iii) is not in itself an objective of budgeting. Although a budget may be set **within a framework of expansion plans**, it is perfectly possible for an organisation to **plan for a reduction in activity.**

Resource allocation (iv) is an objective of budgeting. Most organisations face a situation of **limited resources** and an objective of the budgeting process is to ensure that these resources are allocated among budget centres in the most efficient way.

15.2 C The **principal budget factor** is the factor which limits the activities of an organisation.

Although cash and profit are affected by the level of sales (options A and B), sales is not the only factor which determines the level of cash and profit.

15.3 D The annual budget is set **within the framework of the long-term plan.** It acts as the first step towards the **achievement of the organisation's long-term objectives.** Therefore the long term objectives must be established before any of the other budget tasks can be undertaken and the correct answer is D.

15.4 D The total production cost allowance in a budget flexed at the 83% level of activity would be $8,688 (to the nearest $)
Direct material cost per 1% = $30

Labour and production overhead:

			$
At	90%	activity	6,240
At	80%	activity	6,180
Change	10%		60

Variable cost per 1% activity = $60/10% = $6

Substituting in 80% activity:

Fixed cost of labour and production overhead $\quad = \$6,180 - (80 \times \$6)$
$\qquad\qquad\qquad\qquad\qquad\qquad\qquad\qquad\qquad = \$5,700$

Flexed budget cost allowance:

	$
Direct material $30 × 83	2,490
Labour and production overhead:	
variable $6 × 83	498
fixed	5,700
	8,688

15.5 B   Spreadsheets are not useful for word processing

15.6 B   C4

15.7 C   =D4-D5

15.8 A   =G6/G2*100

15.9 D   Budgeted production = budgeted sales + closing inventory – opening inventory. In March, 10% of March's sales (found in cell F3) will still be inventory at the beginning of the month and 10% of April's sales (cell F4) will be in inventory at the end of the month. Production for March will therefore be

March's sales (F3) + 10% of April's sales (F4) – 10% of March's sales (F3)

Or

=[(0.9*F3) + (0.1*F4)]

15.10 A   They are more time consuming than fixed budgets and they are based on a set of assumptions which may be over simplistic. Managers may not have time available to prepare flexible budgets to cover all possible scenarios. Therefore they will often make simplifying assumptions. They are useful for decision making as they are flexed to the actual level of activity, and therefore allow actual costs to be compared against the standard costs for that actual activity.

16   The budgetary process

16.1 B   The **master budget** is the summary budget into which all subsidiary budgets are consolidated. It usually comprises the **budgeted income statement**, **budgeted balance sheet** and **budgeted cash flow statement**.

The master budget is used **in conjunction with the supporting subsidiary budgets**, to plan and control activities. The subsidiary budgets are not in themselves a part of the master budget. Therefore option D is not correct.

16.2 D   A functional budget is a budget prepared for a particular function or department. A cash budget is **the cash result of the planning decisions included in all the functional budgets**. It is not a functional budget itself. Therefore the correct answer is D.

16.3 B   Since there are no production resource limitations, sales would be the principal budget factor and the sales budget (2) would be prepared first. Budgeted inventory changes included in the finished goods inventory budget (4) would then indicate the required production for the production budget (5). This would lead to the calculation of the material usage (1) which would then be adjusted for the budgeted change in material inventory (6) to determine the required level of budgeted material purchases (3).Therefore the correct answer is B.

16.4 C   Since there are no production resource limitations, sales would be the principal budget factor therefore the sales budget must be prepared before the production budget (1). The budgeted change in finished goods inventory (3) would then indicate the required volume for the production budget. Therefore the correct answer is C.

Item (2), the material purchases, would be information derived **from** the production budget after adjusting for material inventory changes, and item (4), the standard direct labour cost per unit, would be required for the **production cost budget**, but not for the production budget, which is **expressed in volume terms.**

16.5 B Any opening inventory available at the beginning of a period will **reduce** the additional quantity required from production in order to satisfy a given sales volume. Any closing inventory required at the end of a period will **increase** the quantity required from production in order to satisfy sales and leave a sufficient volume in inventory. Therefore we need to **deduct** the opening inventory and **add** the required closing inventory.

16.6 C Once the material usage budget has been prepared, based on the budgeted production volume, the usage is adjusted for the budgeted change in materials inventories in order to determine the required budgeted purchases. If purchases exceed production requirements this means that raw material inventories are being increased, and the correct answer is C.

16.7 C

	Units
Required for sales	24,000
Required to increase inventory (2,000 × 0.25)	500
	24,500

16.8 B

	Units
Required increase in finished goods inventory	1,000
Budgeted sales of Alpha	60,000
Required production	61,000

	kg
Raw materials usage budget (× 3 kg)	183,000
Budgeted decrease in raw materials inventory	(8,000)
Raw materials purchase budget	175,000

16.9 D

	Units
Budgeted sales	18,000
Budgeted reduction in finished goods	(3,600)
Budgeted production of completed units	14,400
Allowance for defective units (10% of output = 1/9 of input)	1,600
Production budget	16,000

16.10 D

	Hours
Active hours required for production = 200 × 6 hours =	1,200
Allowance for idle time (20% of total time = 25% of active time)	300
Total hours to be paid for	1,500
× $7 per hour	
Direct labour cost budget	$10,500

16.11 D

	Units
Planned increase in inventories of finished goods	4,600
Budgeted sales	36,800
Budgeted production (to pass quality control check)	41,400

This is 92% of total production, allowing for an 8% rejection rate.

Budgeted production $= \dfrac{100}{92} \times 41,400 = 45,000$ units

Budgeted direct labour hours = (× 5 hours per unit) 225,000 hours

16.12 D Before you can work out the total cost, you have to determine how many labour hours are required. You can calculate the number of hours required for the units quite easily: 4,800 x 5 = 24,000 hours. However 20% of labour time is idle, which means that 24,000 hours is only 80% of the total hours required to produce 4,800 units. Total hours = 24,000 x (100/80) = 30,000 hours.

Total cost = 30,000 hours x $10 per hour = $300,000 (which is option D)

16.13 D   Statement 1 is true because certain factors are often out of the manager's control. The level of sales (or production) will be out of the manager's control and a flexed budget will account for this. Statement 2 is true. The major purpose of a fixed budget is at the planning stage when it seeks to define the broad objectives of the organisation. Statement 3 is true because forecast volumes are very unlikely to be equal to actual volumes and so the variances will contain large volume differences.

16.14 C   Flexed budgets help managers to deal with uncertainty by allowing them to see the expected outcomes for a range of activity levels. So Statement 1 is true. A flexed budget provides a more meaningful comparison because it shows what costs should have been for the actual level of activity achieved.

17 Making budgets work

17.1 B   Staff suggestions may be ignored leading to de-motivation. Psuedo-participation occurs when managers pretend to involve staff but actually ignore their input. This may lead to a less realistic budget and will certainly be de-motivating if the staff involved find out what is going on.

17.2 C   It is generally agreed that the existence of some form of target or expected outcome is a greater motivation than no target at all. Therefore (1) is true. The establishment of a target, however, raises the question of the degree of difficulty or challenge of the target. Therefore (2) is true. If the performance standard is set too high or too low sub-optimal performance could be the result. The degree of budget difficulty is not easy to establish. It is influenced by the nature of the task, the organisational culture and personality factors. Some people respond positively to a difficult target. Others, if challenged, tend to withdraw their commitment. So (3) is not true.

17.3 C   A budget which is set without permitting the ultimate budget holder to participate in the budgeting process.

17.4 D   Imposed budgets are effective in very small businesses, in newly formed businesses and in times of economic hardship. So A, B and C are not suitable situations. The answer is D.

17.5 A   Participative budgeting should be used in all three circumstances.

17.6 D   A cost which can be influenced by its budget holder.

18 Capital expenditure budgeting

18.1 D   An opportunity cost is the value of the benefit sacrificed when one course of action is chosen, in preference to another.

18.2 C   A decision is about the future, therefore relevant costs are future costs (i). If a cost is unavoidable then any decision taken about the future will not affect the cost, therefore unavoidable costs are not relevant costs (ii). Incremental costs are extra costs which will be incurred in the future therefore relevant costs are incremental costs (iii). Differential costs are the difference in total costs between alternatives and they are therefore affected by a decision taken now and they are associated with relevant costs (iv).

18.3 D

	$
Opportunity cost (net realisable value)	1,200
Cost of disposal in one year's time	800
Total relevant cost of machine	2,000

18.4 C   Purchases of raw materials would be classed as revenue expenditure, not capital expenditure. The others are capital expenditure.

19 Methods of project appraisal

19.1 B Current rate is 6% pa payable monthly

∴ Effective rate is 6/12% = ½% compound every month

∴ In the six months from January to June, interest earned =

($1,000 × [1.005]^6) – $1,000 = $30.38

Option A is incorrect since it is simply 6% × $1,000 = $60 in one year, then divided by 2 to give $30 in six months.

Option C represents the annual interest payable (6% × $1,000 = $60 pa).

Option D is also wrong since this has been calculated (incorrectly) as follows.

$$0.05 \times \$1,000 = \$50 \text{ per month}$$
$$\text{Over six months} = \$50 \times 6$$
$$= \$300 \text{ in six months}$$

19.2 B $2,070 = 115% of the original investment

∴ Original investment $= \dfrac{100}{115} \times \$2,070$

$= \$1,800$

∴ Interest $= \$2,070 - \$1,800$

$= \$270$

Option D is calculated (incorrectly) as follows.

$$\frac{x}{\$2,070} = 15\%$$

∴ x $= 0.15 \times \$2,070$
$= \$310.50$

Make sure that you always tackle this type of question by establishing what the original investment was first.

19.3 C We need to calculate the effective rate of interest.

8% per annum (nominal) is 2% per quarter. The effective annual rate of interest is [1.02^4 – 1] = 0.08243 = 8.243%.

Now we can use S = X(1 + r)^n
S = 12,000 (1.08243)^3
S = $15,218.81

∴ The principal will have grown to approximately $15,219.

19.4 D

		$
PV of $1,200 in one year	= $1,200 × 0.926 =	1,111.20
PV of $1,400 in two years	= $1,400 × 0.857 =	1,199.80
PV of $1,600 in three years	= $1,600 × 0.794 =	1,270.40
PV of $1,800 in four years	= $1,800 × 0.735 =	1,323.00

19.5 D Effective quarterly rate = 1% (4% ÷ 4)
Effective annual rate = [(1.01)^4 – 1]
= 0.0406 = 4.06% pa

You should have been able to eliminate options A and B immediately. 1% is simply 4% ÷ 4 = 1%. 4% is the nominal rate and is therefore not the effective annual rate of interest.

19.6 B   The formula to calculate the IRR is $a\% + \left[\dfrac{A}{A-B} \times (b-a)\right]\%$

where   a = one interest rate
        b = other interest rate
        A = NPV at rate a
        B = NPV at rate b

IRR $= 9\% + \left[\dfrac{22}{22+4} \times 1\right]\%$

$= 9 + 0.85 = 9.85\%$

19.7 B   The discount factor for 10 years at 7% is 0.508.

∴ Original amount invested = $2,000 × 0.508
                           = $1,016

19.8 B   If house prices rise at 2% per calendar month, this is equivalent to

$(1.02)^{12} = 1.268$ or 26.8% per annum

19.9 D   Annuity   = $700

Annuity factor   = 1 + 6.247 (cumulative factor for 9 years, first payment is **now**)
                 = 7.247

$\text{Annuity} = \dfrac{\text{PV of annuity}}{\text{Annuity factor}}$

$\$700 = \dfrac{\text{PV of annuity}}{7.247}$

$700 × 7.247 = PV of annuity
PV of annuity = $5,073 (to the nearest $)

19.10 C   9%

$\text{Annuity} = \dfrac{\text{Present value of annuity}}{\text{Annuity factor}}$

$\text{Annuity factor} = \dfrac{86,400}{19,260}$ $= 4.486$

From tables, this annuity factor corresponds to an interest rate of 9% over six years.

19.11   D

The present value of a perpetuity is:

$PV = \dfrac{a}{r}$

where   a = annuity = $24,000

        r = cost of capital as a proportion   = 5%   = 0.05

∴ PV $= \dfrac{24,000}{0.05}$

$= \$480,000$

19.12   D

The internal rate of return (IRR) of the investment can be calculated using the following formula.

$$IRR = a\% + \left(\frac{A}{A - B} \times (b - a) \right)\%$$

where   a = first interest rate = 12%
         b = second interest rate = 20%
         A = first NPV = $24,000
         B = second NPV = $(8,000)

$$IRR = 12\% + \left(\frac{24,000}{24,000 + 8,000} \times (20 - 12) \right)\%$$

         = 12% + 6%
         = 18%

19.13 D   The non-discounted payback period of Project Beta = 2 years and 6 months.

Workings

Project Beta

Year	Cash inflow	Cumulative cash inflow
	$	$
1	250,000	250,000
2	350,000	600,000
3	400,000	1,000,000
4	200,000	1,200,000
5	150,000	1,350,000
6	150,000	1,500,000

Project Beta has a payback period of between 2 and 3 years.

$$\text{Payback period} = 2 \text{ years} + \left[\frac{\$200,000}{\$400,000} \times 12 \text{ months} \right]$$

         = 2 years + 6 months

19.14 B   The discounted payback period of Project Alpha is between 3 and 4 years.

Workings

Project Alpha

Year	Cash flow	Discount factor	PV	Cum. PV
	$	10%	$	$
0	(800,000)	1.000	(800,000)	(800,000)
1	250,000	0.909	227,250	(572,750)
2	250,000	0.826	206,500	(366,250)
3	400,000	0.751	300,400	(65,850)
4	300,000	0.683	204,900	139,050
5	200,000	0.621	124,200	263,250
6	50,000	0.564	28,200	291,450

The discounted payback period is therefore between three and four years.

19.15 B   The payback period is the time that is required for the total of the cash inflows of a capital investment project to equal the total of the cash outflows, ie initial investment ÷ annual net cash inflow.

19.16 B

	$
Investment	(60,000)
PV of cash inflow	64,600
NPV @ 10%	4,600

	$
Investment	(60,000)
PV of cash inflow	58,200
NPV @ 15%	(1,800)

The IRR of the machine investment is therefore between 10% and 15% because the NPV falls from $4,600 at 10% to –$1,800 at 15%. Therefore at some point between 10% and 15% the NPV = 0. When the NPV = 0, the internal rate of return is reached.

19.17 A   Let x = investment at start of project.

Year	Cash flow $	Discount factor 10%	Present value $
0	x	1.000	(x)
1 – 5	18,000	3.791	68,238
			7,222

∴ –x + $68,238 = $7,222

x = $68,238 – $7,222

x = $61,016

19.18 D   Statements 2 and 4 are true.

19.19 B   IRR is the discount rate at which the net present value of the cash flows from an investment is zero.

19.20 C   At the end of year 3, $74,600 has been 'paid back'. The remaining $15,400 for payback will be received during year 4.

19.21 C $(1.021)^4 - 1 = 0.0867 = 8.67\%$

19.22 C   1,500/0.08 = 18,750

19.23 C   The present value of a perpetuity is:

$$PV = \frac{a}{r}$$

where   a   = annuity = $24,000
         r   = cost of capital as a proportion = 5% = 0.05

$$\therefore PV = \frac{24,000}{0.05}$$

$$= \$480,000$$

20 Standard costing

20.1 B

		$ per unit	$ per unit
Material P	7kg × $4	28	
Material S	3kg × $9	27	
			55
Direct labour	5hr × $7		35
Standard prime cost of product J			90

20.2 B   An attainable standard assumes efficient levels of operation, but includes **allowances** for normal loss, waste and machine downtime.

20.3 C   It is generally accepted that the use of **attainable standards** has the optimum motivational impact on employees. Some allowance is made for unavoidable wastage and inefficiencies, but the attainable level can be reached if production is carried out efficiently.

20.4 D   Required liquid input = 1 litre $\times \dfrac{100}{80}$ = 1.25 litres

20.5 C   When management by exception is operated within a standard costing system, only the variances which exceed acceptable tolerance limits need to be investigated by management with a view to control action. Adverse and favourable variances alike may be subject to investigation, therefore **option A** is incorrect.

Any efficient information system would ensure that only managers who are able to act on the information receive management reports, even if they are not prepared on the basis of management by exception. Therefore **option B** is incorrect.

20.6 A   Standard costing provides targets for achievement, and yardsticks against which actual performance can be monitored (**item 1**). It also provides the unit cost information for evaluating the volume figures contained in a budget (**item 2**). Inventory control systems are simplified with standard costing. Once the variances have been eliminated, all inventory units are valued at standard price (**item 3**).

Item 4 is incorrect because standard costs are an **estimate** of what will happen in the future, and a unit cost target that the organisation is aiming to achieve.

20.7 D   Standard labour cost per unit = 9 hours $\times \dfrac{100}{90} \times \$9 = \$90$

21 Basic variance analysis

21.1 C   Since inventories are valued at standard cost, the material price variance is based on the materials purchased.

	$
12,000 kg material purchased should cost (×$3)	36,000
but did cost	33,600
Material price variance	2,400 (F)

800 units manufactured should use (× 14 kg)	11,200 kg
but did use	11,500 kg
Usage variance in kg	300 kg (A)
× standard price per kg	× $3
Usage variance in $	$900 (A)

21.2 C

	$
2,300 hours should have cost (× $7)	16,100
but did cost	18,600
Rate variance	2,500 (A)

21.3 D

260 units should have taken (× 10 hrs)	2,600 hrs
but took (active hours)	2,200 hrs
Efficiency variance in hours	400 hrs (F)
× standard rate per hour	× $7
Efficiency variance in $	$2,800 (F)

21.4 C   Standard variable production overhead cost per hour = $11,550 ÷ 5,775 = $2

	$
8,280 hours of variable production overhead should cost (× $2)	16,560
but did cost	14,904
Variable production overhead expenditure variance	1,656 (F)

Standard time allowed for one unit = 5,775 hours ÷ 1,925 units = 3 hours

2,070 units should take (× 3 hours)	6,210 hours
but did take	8,280 hours
Efficiency variance in hours	2,070 hours (A)
× standard variable production overhead cost per hour	× $2
Variable production overhead efficiency variance	$4,140 (A)

21.5 C **Fixed overhead expenditure variance**

	$
Budgeted fixed overhead expenditure (4,200 units × $4 per unit)	16,800
Actual fixed overhead expenditure	17,500
Fixed overhead expenditure variance	700 (A)

The variance is adverse because the actual expenditure was higher than the amount budgeted.

Fixed overhead volume variance

	$
Actual production at standard rate (5,000 × $4 per unit)	20,000
Budgeted production at standard rate (4,200 × $4 per unit)	16,800
Fixed overhead volume variance	3,200 (F)

The variance is favourable because the actual volume of output was greater than the budgeted volume of output.

If you selected an incorrect option you misinterpreted the direction of one or both of the variances.

21.6 A

Capacity variance

Budgeted hours of work	9,000 hours
Actual hours of work	9,400 hours
Capacity variance in hours	400 hours (F)
x standard fixed overhead absorption rate per hour *	× $4
Fixed production overhead capacity variance	$1,600 (F)

* $36,000/9,000 = $4 per hour

Efficiency variance

1,900 units of product should take (× 9,000/1,800 hrs)	9,500 hours
but did take	9,400 hours
Efficiency variance in hours	100 hours (F)
x standard fixed overhead absorption rate per hour *	× $4
Fixed production overhead efficiency variance in $	$400 (F)

* $36,000/9,000 = $4 per hour

21.7 C **Statement 1** is not consistent with a favourable labour efficiency variance. Employees of a lower skill level are likely to work less efficiently, resulting in an **adverse efficiency variance**.

Statement 2 is consistent with a favourable labour efficiency variance. **Time would be saved in processing** if the material was easier to process.

Statement 3 is consistent with a favourable labour efficiency variance. **Time would be saved in processing** if working methods were improved.

Therefore the correct answer is C.

21.8 D Direct material cost variance = material price variance + material usage variance

The adverse material usage variance could be larger than the favourable material price variance. The total of the two variances would therefore represent a net result of an adverse total direct material cost variance.

21.9 B

	$
53,000 kg should cost (× $2.50)	132,500
but did cost	136,000
Material price variance	3,500 (A)

21.10 A

	$
27,000 units should use (× 2 kg)	54,000 kg
but did use	53,000 kg
	1,000 kg (F)
x standard cost per kg	2.5
Material usage variance	2,500 (F)

21.11 A

	$
9,200 hours should have cost (× $12.50)	115,000
but did cost	110,750
Direct labour rate variance	4,250 (F)

21.12 D

2,195 units should have taken (× 4 hours)	8,780 hours
but did take	9,200 hours
Direct labour efficiency variance (in hours)	420 hours (A)
x standard rate pre hour	× 12.50
	5,250 (A)

21.13 D

Labour rate variance

	$
14,000 hours should have cost (× $10 per hour)	140,000
but did cost	176,000
Labour rate variance	36,000 (A)

Labour efficiency variance

	$	
5,500 units should have taken (× 3 hours per unit)	16,500	hrs
but did take	14,000	hrs
Labour efficiency variance (in hours)	2,500	hrs (F)
x standard rate per unit	× $10	
	$25,000	(F)

21.14 A

Standard fixed overhead absorption rate per hour = $125,000/25,000 = $5 per hour

Fixed overhead volume capacity variance

Budgeted hours of work	25,000 hrs
Actual hours of work	24,000 hrs
Fixed overhead volume capacity variance	1,000 hrs (A)
x standard fixed overhead absorption rate per hour	× $5
Fixed overhead volume capacity variance in $	$5,000 (A)

21.15 B

The total direct materials variance can be found by comparing the flexed budget figures with the actual figures.

Budgeted material cost per unit	= $110,000/2,200
	= $50
Flexed for 2,000 units	= $50 × 2,000
	= $100,000

Total direct materials variance

	$	
Flexed direct material cost	100,000	
but did cost	110,000	
Total direct materials variance	10,000	(A)

21.16 B

The total direct labour variance can be found by comparing the flexed budget figures with the actual figures.

Budgeted labour cost per unit	= $286,000/2,200
	= $130
Flexed for 2,000 units	= $130 × 2,000
	= $260,000

Total direct labour variance

	$
Flexed direct labour cost	260,000
but did cost	280,000
Total direct labour variance	20,000 (A)

21.17 A

The total direct variable overhead variances can be found by comparing the flexed budget figures with the actual figures.

Budgeted variable overhead cost per unit	= $132,000/2,200
	= $60
Flexed for 2,000 units	= $60 × 2,000
	= $120,000

Total direct variable overhead variance

	$
Flexed direct variable overhead cost	120,000
but did cost	120,000
Total direct variable overhead variance	nil

21.18 A

Statement 1 is true. Statement 2 is false. Producing 5,000 standard hours of work in 5,500 hours would give rise to an adverse fixed overhead volume efficiency variance.

21.19 B

Both statements are true.

22 Further variance analysis

22.1 B

The only fixed overhead variance in a marginal costing statement is the fixed overhead expenditure variance. This is the difference between budgeted and actual overhead expenditure, calculated in the same way as for an absorption costing system.

There is no volume variance with marginal costing, because under or over absorption due to volume changes cannot arise.

22.2 D   Raising prices in response to higher demand would result in a favourable selling price variance.

22.3 A

	$
Total actual direct material cost	2,400
Add back variances: direct material price	(800)
direct material usage	400
Standard direct material cost of production	2,000
Standard material cost per unit	$10
Number of units produced (2,000 ÷ $10)	200

22.4 A

Since there was no change in inventories, the usage variance can be used to calculate the material usage.

Saving in material used compared with standard $= \dfrac{\$400(F)}{\$2 \text{ per kg}} = 200$ kg

Standard material usage for actual production (200 units × 5kg)	1,000 kg
Usage variance in kg	200 kg (F)
Actual usage of material	800 kg

22.5 D

	$
200 units should sell for (× $70)	14,000
but did sell for	15,200
Selling price variance	1,200 (F)

22.6 C   Budgeted sales volume per month $= \dfrac{\text{Budgeted material cost of sales}}{\text{Standard material cost per unit}}$

$= \dfrac{\$2,300}{\$10} = 230$ units

Budgeted profit margin per unit $= \dfrac{\text{Budgeted monthly profit margin}}{\text{Budgeted monthly sales volume}}$

$= \dfrac{\$6,900}{230} = \$30$ per unit

Budgeted sales volume	230 units
Actual sales volume	200 units
Sales volume variance in units	30 units (A)
Standard profit per unit	× $30
Sales volume variance in $	$900 (A)

22.7 B   Actual expenditure = $(48,000 + 2,000) = $50,000
Overhead absorbed = $(50,000 − 8,000) = $42,000
Overhead absorption rate per unit = $48,000 ÷ 4,800 = $10

∴ Number of units produced = $42,000 ÷ $10 = 4,200

22.8 D   Total standard cost of material purchased − actual cost of material purchased = Price variance

Total standard cost	=	$21,920 + $1,370
	=	$23,290
Standard price per kg	=	$23,290/6,850
	=	$3.40

22.9 B

Actual sales	2,550 units
Budgeted sales	2,400 units
Variance in units	150 units (F)
x standard contribution per unit ($(27 − 12))	x $15
Sales volume variance in $	$2,250 (F)

	$
Revenue from 2,550 units should have been (× $27)	68,850
but was	67,320
Selling price variance	1,530 (A)

22.10 C

	$	
Budgeted sales volume	10,000	units
Actual sales volume	9,800	units
Sales volume variance (units)	200	units (A)
x standard profit per unit	x $5	
Sales volume profit variance (in $)	$1,000	(A)

22.11 B   **Direct material price variance**

	$
12,000 litres should have cost (x $2.50)	30,000
But did cost (12,000 x $2.50 x 1.04)	31,200
Direct material price variance	1,200 (A)

22.12 C   Standard cost per unit = 10.5 litres x $2.50 per litre

= $26.25 per unit

Standard cost of actual production = standard cost + variance
= $(12,000 litres x $2.50) + 1,815
= $(30,000 + 1,815)
= $31,815

∴ Actual production = standard cost of actual production/standard cost per unit

= 31,815/$26.25

= 1,212 units

22.13 C

	$
Sales revenue for 9,000 units should have been (× $12.50)	112,500
but was	117,000
Sales price variance	4,500 (F)

22.14 C

	$
8,500 units should have cost (× $15)	127,500
but did cost (8,500 × $17)	144,500
	17,000 (A)

22.15 B

	$
Absorbed overhead (12,400 × 1.02 × $4.25)	53,754
Actual overhead	56,389
Under-absorbed overhead	2,635

22.16 D

	$
Standard contribution	10,000
Sales price variance	500
Variable cost variance	(2,000)
	8,500

22.17 D   The sales volume variance in a marginal costing system is valued at standard contribution per unit, rather than standard profit per unit.

Contribution per unit of E = $15 – $8 = $7

Sales volume variance in terms of contribution = $\dfrac{\$9,000(A)}{\$5} \times \$7 = \$12,600$ (A)

22.18 B   Closing inventory valuation under absorption costing will always be higher than under marginal costing because of the absorption of fixed overheads into closing inventory values.

The profit under absorption costing will be greater because the fixed overhead being carried forward in closing inventory is greater than the fixed overhead being written off in opening inventory.

22.19 A   If marginal costing is used to value inventory instead of absorption costing, the difference in profits will be equal to the change in inventory volume multiplied by the fixed production overhead absorption rate = 80 units x $34 = $2,720

Since closing inventory are higher than opening inventories, the marginal costing profit will be lower that the absorption costing profit (so **option B** is incorrect). This is because the marginal costing profit does not 'benefit' from the increase in the amount of fixed production overhead taken to inventory (rather than to the income statement).

If you selected **options C or D** you based the difference on 100 units of opening inventory.

22.20 B   Marginal costing:

	$'000	$'000
Sales (25,000 x $80)		2,000
Opening inventory		
Variable production overhead (W1)	1,560	
	1,560	
Less closing inventory (W2)		
Variable cost of sales		1,500
Contribution		500
Less fixed costs (W3)		182
Profit		318

Workings

(1)   26,000 units x $60 = $1,560,000

(2)   Production units + opening inventory – sales   = closing inventory
         = 26,000 + 0 – 25,000 = 1,000 units

    Valued at marginal cost: 1,000 x $60   = $60,000

(3)   Fixed production overhead + fixed selling costs   = $113,000 + $69,000 = $182,000

> Alternative approach
>
> | | $'000 |
> |---|---|
> | Total contribution (25,000 × $20 (W1)) | 500 |
> | Less fixed production overhead | (113) |
> | Less fixed selling costs | (69) |
> | MC profit | 318 |
>
> Workings
>
> 1 contribution per unit = $80-$60 = $20

22.21 C   Absorption costing

OAR = Budgeted overhead / budgeted production = $143,000/26,000 = $5.5/unit

As inventory has increased, absorption costing will report a higher profit than marginal costing.

The difference in profit	=	change in inventory volume × fixed production overhead per unit
	=	1,000 × $5.5
	=	$5,500

Marginal profit	=	$318,000
∴ absorption profit	=	$318,000 + $5,500 = $323,500

22.22 B   Standard marginal costing reconciliation

	$
Original budgeted contribution	290,000
Sales volume variance	(36,250)
Standard contribution from actual sales	253,750
Selling price variance	21,875
	275,625
Variable cost variances	
Total direct material variance	(6,335)
Total direct labour variance	11,323
Total variable overhead variance	(21,665)
Actual contribution	258,948

23 Performance measurement

23.1 B   Attainable (which is part of the SMART objectives framework) is different from 'easily achievable'. The objectives should be motivational which means that they should be at least a little bit challenging.

23.2 C   Cashflow information is a financial performance measure. Options A, B and D are all non-financial indicators (NFIs).

23.3 C   Efficiency

23.4 D   Factors fundamental to strategic success

23.5 A   Acid test ratio $= \dfrac{\text{Current assets} - \text{inventory}}{\text{Current liabilities}}$

$= \dfrac{40,000 + 1,250}{60,000}$

$= 0.6875$

23.6 A   The mission statement gives the purpose and strategy of the organisation. The business will then use this as a focus for setting appropriate objectives.

23.7 C   1, 2 and 4 only. The mission states the aims of the organisation. The strategy outlines what the organisation should be doing; the values and the policies set limits to the ways the strategy may be converted into performance. Profitability is an objective and relates to the critical success factors for business success.

23.8 A   Reducing training costs may mean that the business is faced with a skills shortage in the long term. 2, 3 and 4 should all benefit the business in the long term.

23.9 A   Both are true.

23.10 C   It is when there is a bias towards short term rather than long term performance. Longer term objectives are sacrificed.

23.11 C CO_2 emissions are probably more likely to be measured because of government legislation. They are not one of the usual measures of performance (depending on the industry).

23.12 A   Both statements are true.

24 Applications of performance measures

24.1 A   Return on investment $= \dfrac{\text{Profit}}{\text{Capital employed}} \times 100\%$

        For 20X7 ROI $= \dfrac{7,500}{37,500} \times 100\% = 20\%$

        For 20X8 ROI $= \dfrac{9,000}{60,000} \times 100\% = 15\%$

24.2 C   Asset turnover $= \dfrac{\text{Sales}}{\text{Capital employed}}$

$$= \dfrac{450,000}{60,000}$$

$$= 7.5 \text{ times}$$

24.3 C   Profit is a measure that most non-financial managers can understand, which raises rather than reduces its popularity in business. Option A supports the criticism because customers are often omitted from consideration. (Their interests can be accounted for using a model such as the balanced scorecard.) Option B means that expenditure on intangible assets such as training, marketing and R&D is discouraged. This can have an adverse effect on a business's long term prospects. Option D means that profit is less reliable as a performance measure.

24.4 B   Effectiveness can only be measured in terms of achieved performance. Economy consists of minimising costs, for example, by obtaining suitable inputs at the lowest price. Efficiency, in the narrow sense used here, consists of achieving the greatest output per unit of input: avoiding waste of inputs would contribute to this. Achieving a given level of profit is a measure of overall efficiency in its wider sense and would require proper attention to all three of these matters.

24.5 D   Level of refunds given. The level of refunds given should be used in the customer perspective. If Balance Co has to offer a high level of refunds, this is likely to indicate a low level of customer satisfaction with its product.

24.6 A   The number of customer complaints and the number of repeat orders as a proportion of total orders will reflect the quality of service customers feel they have received from the business. Although sales volume will be affected by the business's ability to retain customers, increasing sales is a more direct measure of the business's marketing effectiveness than its service quality.

24.7 B   1, 2 and 3 are non-financial objectives.

24.8 D   Statement 1 is true. If performance measurement systems focus entirely on those items which can be expressed in monetary terms, managers will concentrate on those variables and ignore other important variables that cannot be expressed in monetary terms. Statement 2 is true. Statement 3 is also true, Financial performance indicators have been said to simply measure success. What organisations require, however, are performance indicators that ensure success. Such indicators, linked to an organisation's critical success factors such as quality and flexibility, will be non-financial in nature.

24.9 D   Staff turnover. A, B and C are performance measures of service quality. D is a performance measure of human resources.

24.10 B   The ROI target is 13% and the cost of capital is 12%. The ROI is calculated as $30,000/$200,000 × 100% = 15% and so the project would be accepted. The RI is calculated as $30,000 – (12% × $200,000) = $6,000. The project would be accepted.

24.11 D   1, 2 and 3. The figures needed to calculate ROI are easily available from the financial accounting records.

24.12 C   Variance analysis and defective units would be more appropriate for manufacturing organisations with large production volumes.

24.13 A   Relative market share is usually a measure of competitiveness. Efficiency and productivity are measures of resource utilisation.

24.14 B   Cost per consignment. Number of customer complaints and client evaluation interviews would be measures of quality. Depot profit league tables is a measure of profit.

25 Cost management

25.1 B   Work study

25.2 B   1 and 2 only. Value analysis focuses on costs, not sales volumes or prices

26 Mixed Bank 1

26.1 C

	$ per unit
Material	20.00
Labour	69.40
Production overhead (14 hours × $12.58)	176.12
Total production cost	265.52
General overhead (8% × $265.52)	21.24
	286.76

26.2 A

		Process 1		Process 2
		kg		kg
Input		47,000		42,000
Normal loss	(× 8%)	3,760	(× 5%)	2,100
Expected output		43,240		39,900
Actual output		42,000		38,915
Abnormal loss		1,240		985

26.3 C   The actual sales revenue is higher than the flexed budget sales revenue. Since the effect of a sales volume change has been removed from this comparison the higher revenue must be caused by a higher than standard selling price.

26.4 A   Variable costs are conventionally deemed to increase or decrease in direct proportion to changes in output. Therefore the correct answer is A. Descriptions B and D imply a changing unit rate, which does not comply with this convention. Description C relates to a fixed cost.

26.5 D   None of the criticisms apply in *all* circumstances.

Criticism (i) has some validity but even where output is not standardised it may be possible to identify a number of standard components and activities whose costs may be controlled effectively by the use of standard costs.

Criticism (ii) also has some validity but the use of information technology means that standards can be updated rapidly and more frequently, so that they may be useful for the purposes of control by comparison.

Criticism (iii) can also be addressed in some circumstances. The use of ideal standards and more demanding performance levels can combine the benefits of continuous improvement and standard costing control.

26.6 A   Capital expenditure is the cost of acquiring or enhancing non-current assets.

26.7 D

	A	B	C	D
Overhead expenditure	18,757	29,025	46,340	42,293
Direct labour hours	3,080	6,750		
Machine hours			3,380	2,640
Overhead absorption rate	$6.09	$4.30	$13.71	$16.02

26.8 C   Production cost per unit = $3.60 + ($258,000/60,000) = $7.90

Profit = 700,000 – (56,000 × 7.90) – 144,000 = $113,600

	$	$
Revenue		700,000
Production costs:		
Variable		
(56,000 + 4,000) × $3.60	216,000	
Fixed	258,000	
Closing stock (4,000 × $7.90)	(31,600)	
		(442,200)
		257,600
Fixed non-production costs		(144,000)
		113,600

26.9   C   Inventory levels have increased so marginal costing will result in higher profits and lower inventory values than absorption costing.

26.10 D   A by-product can be defined as being 'output of some value, produced incidentally while manufacturing the main product'.

Option A is incorrect because a by-product has some value.

Option B is incorrect because this description could also apply to a joint product.

Option C is incorrect because the value of the product described could be relatively high, even though the output volume is relatively low.

26.11 B

	A	B	C	D
	$	$	$	$
Variable manufacturing costs	6.00	8.00	9.00	11.50
Bought-in price	11.00	11.50	13.00	16.00
Difference	5.00	3.50	4.00	4.50

Component B has the lowest difference between the cost of manufacture and the cost of buying it in. This would therefore have the smallest effect on profit.

26.12 A $$IRR = a\% + [\frac{A}{A-B} \times (b-a)]\%$$

where a is one interest rate
       b is the other interest rate
       A is the NPV at rate a
       B is the NPV at rate b

$$IRR = 14\% + \left[\frac{16,000}{(16,000+10,500)} \times (20-14)\right]\%$$

= 14% + 3.6%

= 17.6%

26.13 C   Present value = $8,000 + ($8,000 × 3.791) = $38,328

26.14 C   Lowering the selling price by 15% is best described as a short term tactical plan.

26.15 B   Fixed costs per unit $= \$16 \div 4 = \$4$

Units in closing inventory $= 17,500 - 15,000 = 2,500$ units

Profit difference   = inventory increase in units x fixed overhead per unit
                              $= 2,500 \times \$4 = \$10,000$

Inventories increased, therefore fixed overhead would have been carried forward in inventory using absorption costing and the profit would be higher than with marginal costing.

If you selected **option A** you calculated the correct profit difference, but misinterpreted the 'direction' of the difference.
If you **selected option C** or **D** you evaluated the inventory difference at variable cost and full cost respectively.

26.16 C   Total purchase costs = annual demand x purchase price

$= 20,000 \times \$40$ per unit

$= \$800,000$

Order costs

Number of orders $= \dfrac{\text{Annual demand}}{\text{EOQ}} = \dfrac{20,000\,\text{units}}{500\,\text{units}} = 40$ orders per annum

Cost per   = 40 orders x \$25 per order

Total order costs = \$1,000

Holding costs

Average inventory held $=$ EOQ/2 $= 500/2 = 250$ units

It costs \$4 to hold each unit of inventory

$\therefore$ Holding costs = average inventory held $\times$ \$4 per unit

$= 250$ units $\times$ \$4 per unit $= \$1,000$

Total annual costs of inventory

	$
Purchase costs	800,000
Order costs	1,000
Holding costs	1,000
Total	802,000

26.17 B   The least squares method of linear regression analysis involves using the following formulae for a and b in $Y = a + bX$.

$$b = \frac{n\Sigma XY - \Sigma X\Sigma Y}{n\Sigma X^2 - (\Sigma X)^2}$$

$$= \frac{(5 \times 8,104) - (100 \times 400)}{(5 \times 2,040) - 100^2}$$

$$= \frac{40,520 - 40,000}{10,200 - 10,000}$$

$$= \frac{520}{200}$$

$$= 2.6$$

At this stage, you can eliminate options A and C.

$$a = \frac{\Sigma Y}{n} - b\frac{\Sigma X}{b}$$

157

$$= \frac{400}{5} - 2.6 \times (\frac{100}{5})$$

$$= 28.$$

26.18 A

	Recruit $'000	Retrain $'000
4 new employees (4 × $40,000)	160	
Training cost		15
Replacements		100
	160	115

The supervision cost would be incurred anyway and is not a relevant cost, since an existing manager is used. Similarly, the salaries of the existing employees are not relevant.

The lowest cost option is to retrain the existing employees, at a total relevant cost of $115,000. Therefore the correct answer is A.

26.19 C 0.17

$$r = \frac{n\Sigma xy - \Sigma x \Sigma y}{\sqrt{[n\Sigma x^2 - (\Sigma x)^2][n\Sigma y^2 - (\Sigma y)^2]}}$$

$$= \frac{(6 \times 14) - (2 \times 15)}{\sqrt{[6 \times 30 - 2^2][6 \times 130 - 15^2]}} = \frac{84 - 30}{\sqrt{176 \times 555}} = \frac{54}{312.54} = 0.172778 = 0.17$$

(to 2 dec places)

26.20 C The total cost of the job is $440 (to the nearest $)

	$
Direct materials 10kg × $10	100
Direct labour 20 hours × $5	100
Prime cost	200
Variable production overhead 20 hours × $2	40
Fixed production overhead 20 hours × $10*	200
Total production cost	440
Selling, distribution and administration	50
Total cost	490

* Overhead absorption rate = $\dfrac{\$100,000}{10,000}$ = $10 per labour hour

27 Mixed Bank 2

27.1 B A target of providing at least 40 hours of training every year to improve skills and productivity has a learning and growth perspective.

27.2 C Trend, seasonal variation and cyclical variation

27.3 B Profit before interest and tax ÷ (Ordinary shareholders' funds + Non-current liabilities) × 100

27.4 B ($20,000 × 20%) – ($8,000 × 10%) = $3,200

27.5 A Direct labour and variable production overhead

27.6 C Let x = the number of hours 12,250 units should have taken

12,250 units should have taken	x hrs
but did take	41,000 hrs
Labour efficiency variance (in hrs)	x – 41,000 hrs

Labour efficiency variance (in $) = $11,250 (F)

∴ Labour efficiency variance (in hrs) $= \dfrac{\$11,250\,(F)}{\$6}$

= 1,875 (F)

∴ 1,875 hrs = (x – 41,000) hrs

∴ standard hours for 12,250 units = 41,000 + 1,875

= 42,875 hrs

∴ Standard hours per unit $= \dfrac{42{,}875\ hrs}{12{,}250\ units}$

= 3.50 hrs

If you selected **option A** you treated the efficiency variance as adverse. **Option B** is the actual hours taken per unit and **option D** is the figure for the standard wage rate per hour.

27.7 C ($200,000 + ((100,000 – 80,000) X $5) = $300,000

27.8 B ((1,440 X 120 ÷ 240 ÷ 600) – 1) X 100 = 20%

27.9 A They are *not* an efficient method of storing text based files.

27.10 A (6,000 units – 5,000 units) X $25,000 ÷ 5,000 units

27.11 A It recognises that overhead costs are not always driven by the volume of production

27.12 A $IRR = a\% + [\,\dfrac{A}{A-B} \times (b - a)]\%$

where a is one interest rate
  b is the other interest rate
  A is the NPV at rate a
  B is the NPV at rate b

IRR = 14% + [(16,000/(16,000+10,500)) X 6%
= 14% + 3.6%
= 17.6%

27.13 A Adverse fixed overhead capacity variance

27.14 D

Current ratio	Liquidity
Reduce by 10%	Reduce by 20%

27.15 D Cluster sampling

27.16 C (5,000 × $12 × 20 ÷ 120) + 8,000 = $18,000

27.17 C $57,200 − (5,200 × $50,000 ÷ 5,000 units) = $5,200 favourable

27.18 A   (5,200 units − 5,000 units) × $20,000 ÷ 5,000 units = $800

27.19 A   The variable cost per unit.

27.20 B   RI will increase and ROI will decrease.

Formula sheet given in the exam

Regression analysis

$y = a + bx$

$$a = \frac{\Sigma Y}{n} - \frac{b\Sigma x}{n}$$

$$b = \frac{n\Sigma xy - \Sigma x \Sigma y}{n\Sigma x^2 - (\Sigma x)^2}$$

$$r = \frac{n\Sigma xy - \Sigma x \Sigma y}{\sqrt{(n\Sigma x^2 - (\Sigma x)^2)(n\Sigma y^2 - (\Sigma y)^2)}}$$

Economic order quantity

$$\sqrt{\frac{2C_0 D}{C_h}}$$

Economic batch quantity

$$\sqrt{\frac{2C_0 D}{C_h(1 - \frac{D}{R})}}$$

Present value table

Present value of £1 ie $(1+r)^{-n}$

where r = interest rate,

n = number of periods until payment

Periods	Discount rates (r)									
(n)	1%	2%	3%	4%	5%	6%	7%	8%	9%	10%
1	0.990	0.980	0.971	0.962	0.952	0.943	0.935	0.926	0.917	0.909
2	0.980	0.961	0.943	0.925	0.907	0.890	0.873	0.857	0.842	0.826
3	0.971	0.942	0.915	0.889	0.864	0.840	0.816	0.794	0.772	0.751
4	0.961	0.924	0.888	0.855	0.823	0.792	0.763	0.735	0.708	0.683
5	0.951	0.906	0.863	0.822	0.784	0.747	0.713	0.681	0.650	0.621
6	0.942	0.888	0.837	0.790	0.746	0.705	0.666	0.630	0.596	0.564
7	0.933	0.871	0.813	0.760	0.711	0.665	0.623	0.583	0.547	0.513
8	0.923	0.853	0.789	0.731	0.677	0.627	0.582	0.540	0.502	0.467
9	0.914	0.837	0.766	0.703	0.645	0.592	0.544	0.500	0.460	0.424
10	0.905	0.820	0.744	0.676	0.614	0.558	0.508	0.463	0.422	0.386
11	0.896	0.804	0.722	0.650	0.585	0.527	0.475	0.429	0.388	0.350
12	0.887	0.788	0.701	0.625	0.557	0.497	0.444	0.397	0.356	0.319
13	0.879	0.773	0.681	0.601	0.530	0.469	0.415	0.368	0.326	0.290
14	0.870	0.758	0.661	0.577	0.505	0.442	0.388	0.340	0.299	0.263
15	0.861	0.743	0.642	0.555	0.481	0.417	0.362	0.315	0.275	0.239

(n)	11%	12%	13%	14%	15%	16%	17%	18%	19%	20%
1	0.901	0.893	0.885	0.877	0.870	0.862	0.855	0.847	0.840	0.833
2	0.812	0.797	0.783	0.769	0.756	0.743	0.731	0.718	0.706	0.694
3	0.731	0.712	0.693	0.675	0.658	0.641	0.624	0.609	0.593	0.579
4	0.659	0.636	0.613	0.592	0.572	0.552	0.534	0.516	0.499	0.482
5	0.593	0.567	0.543	0.519	0.497	0.476	0.456	0.437	0.419	0.402
6	0.535	0.507	0.480	0.456	0.432	0.410	0.390	0.370	0.352	0.335
7	0.482	0.452	0.425	0.400	0.376	0.354	0.333	0.314	0.296	0.279
8	0.434	0.404	0.376	0.351	0.327	0.305	0.285	0.266	0.249	0.233
9	0.391	0.361	0.333	0.308	0.284	0.263	0.243	0.225	0.209	0.194
10	0.352	0.322	0.295	0.270	0.247	0.227	0.208	0.191	0.176	0.162
11	0.317	0.287	0.261	0.237	0.215	0.195	0.178	0.162	0.148	0.135
12	0.286	0.257	0.231	0.208	0.187	0.168	0.152	0.137	0.124	0.112
13	0.258	0.229	0.204	0.182	0.163	0.145	0.130	0.116	0.104	0.093
14	0.232	0.205	0.181	0.160	0.141	0.125	0.111	0.099	0.088	0.078
15	0.209	0.183	0.160	0.140	0.123	0.108	0.095	0.084	0.074	0.065

Annuity table

Present value of an annuity of 1 ie $\dfrac{1-(1+r)^{-n}}{r}$.

where r = interest rate,

n = number of periods

Periods (n)	Discount rates (r)									
	1%	2%	3%	4%	5%	6%	7%	8%	9%	10%
1	0.990	0.980	0.971	0.962	0.952	0.943	0.935	0.926	0.917	0.909
2	1.970	1.942	1.913	1.886	1.859	1.833	1.808	1.783	1.759	1.736
3	2.941	2.884	2.829	2.775	2.723	2.673	2.624	2.577	2.531	2.487
4	3.902	3.808	3.717	3.630	3.546	3.465	3.387	3.312	3.240	3.170
5	4.853	4.713	4.580	4.452	4.329	4.212	4.100	3.993	3.890	3.791
6	5.795	5.601	5.417	5.242	5.076	4.917	4.767	4.623	4.486	4.355
7	6.728	6.472	6.230	6.002	5.786	5.582	5.389	5.206	5.033	4.868
8	7.652	7.325	7.020	6.733	6.463	6.210	5.971	5.747	5.535	5.335
9	8.566	8.162	7.786	7.435	7.108	6.802	6.515	6.247	5.995	5.759
10	9.471	8.983	8.530	8.111	7.722	7.360	7.024	6.710	6.418	6.145
11	10.368	9.787	9.253	8.760	8.306	7.887	7.499	7.139	6.805	6.495
12	11.255	10.575	9.954	9.385	8.863	8.384	7.943	7.536	7.161	6.814
13	12.134	11.348	10.635	9.986	9.394	8.853	8.358	7.904	7.487	7.103
14	13.004	12.106	11.296	10.563	9.899	9.295	8.745	8.244	7.786	7.367
15	13.865	12.849	11.938	11.118	10.380	9.712	9.108	8.559	8.061	7.606

(n)	11%	12%	13%	14%	15%	16%	17%	18%	19%	20%
1	0.901	0.893	0.885	0.877	0.870	0.862	0.855	0.847	0.840	0.833
2	1.713	1.690	1.668	1.647	1.626	1.605	1.585	1.566	1.547	1.528
3	2.444	2.402	2.361	2.322	2.283	2.246	2.210	2.174	2.140	2.106
4	3.102	3.037	2.974	2.914	2.855	2.798	2.743	2.690	2.639	2.589
5	3.696	3.605	3.517	3.433	3.352	3.274	3.199	3.127	3.058	2.991
6	4.231	4.111	3.998	3.889	3.784	3.685	3.589	3.498	3.410	3.326
7	4.712	4.564	4.423	4.288	4.160	4.039	3.922	3.812	3.706	3.605
8	5.146	4.968	4.799	4.639	4.487	4.344	4.207	4.078	3.954	3.837
9	5.537	5.328	5.132	4.946	4.772	4.607	4.451	4.303	4.163	4.031
10	5.889	5.650	5.426	5.216	5.019	4.833	4.659	4.494	4.339	4.192
11	6.207	5.938	5.687	5.453	5.234	5.029	4.836	4.656	4.486	4.327
12	6.492	6.194	5.918	5.660	5.421	5.197	4.988	4.793	4.611	4.439
13	6.750	6.424	6.122	5.842	5.583	5.342	5.118	4.910	4.715	4.533
14	6.982	6.628	6.302	6.002	5.724	5.468	5.229	5.008	4.802	4.611
15	7.191	6.811	6.462	6.142	5.847	5.575	5.324	5.092	4.876	4.675

Mock Exam 1
(Pilot Paper)

FIA/ACCA
FMA/F2
Management Accounting

Mock Examination 1
(Pilot Paper)

Question Paper	
Time allowed	2 hours
ALL FIFTY questions are compulsory and MUST be answered	

DO NOT OPEN THIS PAPER UNTIL YOU ARE READY TO START UNDER EXAMINATION CONDITIONS

ALL 50 questions are compulsory and MUST be attempted

Each question is worth 2 marks.

1   A manufacturing company benchmarks the performance of its accounts receivable department with that of a leading credit card company.

What type of benchmarking is the company using?

A   Internal benchmarking
B   Competitive benchmarking
C   Functional benchmarking
D   Strategic benchmarking   **(2 marks)**

2   Which of the following BEST describes target costing?

A   Setting a cost by subtracting a desired profit margin from a competitive market price
B   Setting a price by adding a desired profit margin to a production cost
C   Setting a cost for the use in the calculation of variances
D   Setting a selling price for the company to aim for in the long run   **(2 marks)**

3   Information relating to two processes (F and G) was as follows:

Process	Normal loss as	Input	Output
	% of input	(litres)	(litres)
F	8	65,000	58,900
G	5	37,500	35,700

For each process, was there an abnormal loss or an abnormal gain?

	Process F	Process G
A	Abnormal gain	Abnormal gain
B	Abnormal gain	Abnormal loss
C	Abnormal loss	Abnormal gain
D	Abnormal loss	Abnormal loss

(2 marks)

4   The following budgeted information relates to a manufacturing company for next period:

	Units		$
Production	14,000	Fixed production costs	63,000
Sales	12,000	Fixed selling costs	12,000

The normal level of activity is 14,000 units per period.

Using absorption costing the profit for next period has been calculated as $36,000

What would be the profit for next period using marginal costing?

A $25,000
B $27,000
C $45,000
D $47,000   **(2 marks)**

5   A company has a budgeted material cost of $125,000 for the production of 25,000 units per month. Each unit is budgeted to use 2 kg of material. The standard cost of material is $2•50 per kg. Actual materials in the month cost $136,000 for 27,000 units and 53,000 kg were purchased and used.

What was the adverse material price variance?

A $1,000
B $3,500
C $7,500
D $11,000   **(2 marks)**

6   Under which sampling method does every member of the target population have an equal chance of being in the sample?

A   Stratified sampling
B   Random sampling
C   Systematic sampling
D   Cluster sampling   **(2 marks)**

7   The following statements refer to spreadsheets:

(1) A spreadsheet is the most suitable software for the storage of large volume of data
(2) A spreadsheet could be used to produce a flexible budget
(3) Most spreadsheets contain a facility to display the data within them in a graphical form

Which of these statements are correct?

A   1 and 2 only
B   1 and 3 only
C   2 and 3 only
D   1, 2 and 3   **(2 marks)**

8   Up to a given level of activity in each period the purchase price per unit of a raw material is constant. After that point a lower price per unit applies both to further units purchased and also retrospectively to all units already purchased.

Which of the following graphs depicts the total cost of the raw materials for a period?

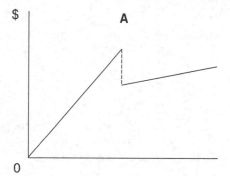 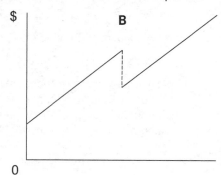

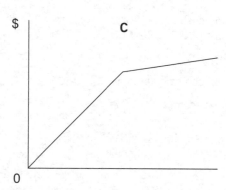 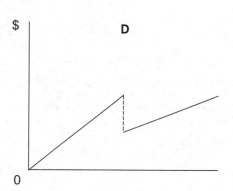

A   Graph A
B   Graph B
C   Graph C
D   Graph D   **(2 marks)**

9   Which of the following are benefits of budgeting?

1   It helps coordinate the activities of different departments
2   It fulfils legal reporting obligations
3   It establishes a system of control
4   It is a starting point for strategic planning

A   1 and 4 only
B   1 and 3 only
C   2 and 3 only
D   2 and 4 only   **(2 marks)**

10   The following statements relate to the participation of junior management in setting budgets:

1   It speeds up the setting of budgets
2   It increases the motivation of junior managers
3   It reduces the level of budget padding

Which statements are true?

A   1 only
B   2 only
C   2 and 3 only
D   1, 2 and 3   **(2 marks)**

11   A company has a capital employed of $200,000. It has a cost of capital of 12% per year. Its residual income is $36,000.

What is the company's return on investment?

A   30%
B   12%
C   18%
D   22%   **(2 marks)**

12   A company has calculated a $10,000 adverse direct material variance by subtracting its flexed budget direct material cost from its actual direct material cost for the period.

Which of the following could have caused the variance?

(1)   An increase in direct material prices
(2)   An increase in raw material usage per unit
(3)   Units produced being greater than budgeted
(4)   Units sold being greater than budgeted

A   2 and 3 only
B   3 and 4 only
C   1 and 2 only
D   1 and 4 only   **(2 marks)**

13   An organisation has the following total costs at two activity levels:

Activity level (units)	16,000	22,000
Total costs ($)	135,000	170,000

Variable costs per unit is constant within this range of activity but there is a step up of $5,000 in the total fixed costs when the activity exceeds 17,500 units.

What is the total cost at an activity level of 20,000 units?

A $163,320
B $158,320
C $160,000
D $154,545   **(2 marks)**

14   Which of the following are suitable measures of performance at the strategic level?

(1)   Return on investment
(2)   Market share
(3)   Number of customer complaints

A   1 and 2
B   2 only
C   2 and 3
D   1 and 3   (2 marks)

15   Which of the following are feasible values for the correlation coefficient?

1   +1.40
2   +1.04
3   0
4   −0.94

A   1 and 2 only
B   3 and 4 only
C   1, 2 and 4 only
D   1, 2, 3 and 4   (2 marks)

16   A company's operating costs are 60% variable and 40% fixed.

Which of the following variances' values would change if the company switched from standard marginal costing to standard absorption costing?

A   Direct material efficiency variance
B   Variable overhead efficiency variance
C   Sales volume variance
D   Fixed overhead expenditure variance   (2 marks)

17   ABC Co has a manufacturing capacity of 10,000 units. The flexed production cost budget of the company is as follows:

Capacity 60% 100% Total production costs $11,280 $15,120

What is the budgeted total production cost if it operates at 85% capacity?

A $13,680
B $12,852
C $14,025
D $12,340   (2 marks)

18   Using an interest rate of 10% per year the net present value (NPV) of a project has been correctly calculated as $50. If the interest rate is increased by 1% the NPV of the project falls by $20.

What is the internal rate of return (IRR) of the project?

A   7.5%
B   11.7%
C   12.5%
D   20.0%   (2 marks)

19   Which of the following BEST describes a principle budget factor?

A   A factor that affects all budget centres
B   A factor that is controllable by a budget centre manager
C   A factor that the management accountant builds into all budgets
D   A factor which limits the activities of an organisation   (2 marks)

20   A company always determines its order quantity for a raw material by using the Economic Order Quantity (EOQ) model.

What would be the effects on the EOQ and the total annual holding cost of a decrease in the cost of ordering a batch of raw material?

	EOQ	Annual holding cost
A	Higher	Lower
B	Higher	Higher
C	Lower	Higher
D	Lower	Lower

(2 marks)

21   A company which operates a process costing system had work-in-progress at the start of last month of 300 units (valued at $1,710) which were 60% complete in respect of all costs. Last month a total of 2,000 units were completed and transferred to the finished goods warehouse. The cost per equivalent unit for costs arising last month was $10. The company uses the FIFO method of cost allocation.

What was the total value of the 2,000 units transferred to the finished goods warehouse last month?

A $19,910
B $20,000
C $20,510
D $21,710

(2 marks)

22   A manufacturing company operates a standard absorption costing system. Last month 25,000 production hours were budgeted and the budgeted fixed production cost was $125,000. Last month the actual hours worked were 24,000 and standard hours for actual production were 27,000.

What was the fixed production overhead capacity variance for last month?

A $5,000 Adverse
B $5,000 Favourable
C $10,000 Adverse
D $10,000 Favourable

(2 marks)

23   The following statements have been made about value analysis.

(1)   It seeks the lowest cost method of achieving a desired function
(2)   It always results in inferior products
(3)   It ignores esteem value
(4)   It is applicable to both physical products and services

Which TWO of the above statements are true?

A   1 and 4
B   1 and 2
C   3 and 4
D   2 and 3

(2 marks)

24

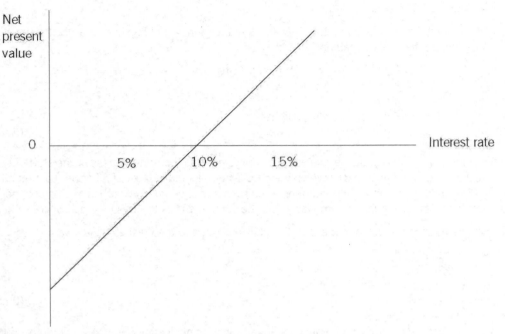

Which of the following is correct with regard to the above graph?

(1)   The IRR is 10%
(2)   The NPV at 15% is positive
(3)   The project's total inflows exceed the total outflows

A   1 and 2 only
B   1 and 3 only
C   2 and 3 only
D   1,2 and 3   **(2 marks)**

25   A company uses standard absorption costing. The following data relate to last month:

	Budget	Actual
Sales and production (units)	1,000	900
	Standard ($)	Actual ($)
Selling price per unit	50	52
Total production cost per unit	39	40

What was the adverse sales volume profit variance last month?

A $1,000
B $1,100
C $1,200
D $1,300   **(2 marks)**

26   The following statements relate to the advantages that linear regression analysis has over the high low method in the analysis of cost behaviour:

1.   the reliability of the analysis can be statistically tested
2.   it takes into account all of the data
3.   it assumes linear cost behaviour

Which statements are true?

A   1 only
B   1 and 2 only
C   2 and 3 only
D   1, 2 and 3   **(2 marks)**

27 Mr Manaton has recently won a competition where he has the choice between receiving $5,000 now or an annual amount forever starting now (i.e. a level perpetuity starting immediately). The interest rate is 8% per annum.

What would be the value of the annual perpetuity to the nearest $?

A $370
B $500
C $400
D $620   **(2 marks)**

28 Which of the following would not be expected to appear in an organisation's mission statement?

A The organisation's values and beliefs
B The products or services offered by the organisation
C Quantified short term targets the organisation seeks to achieve
D The organisation's major stakeholders   **(2 marks)**

29 An organisation operates a piecework system of remuneration, but also guarantees its employees 80% of a time-based rate of pay which is based on $20 per hour for an eight hour working day. Three minutes is the standard time allowed per unit of output. Piecework is paid at the rate of $18 per standard hour.

If an employee produces 200 units in eight hours on a particular day, what is the employee's gross pay for that day?

A $128
B $144
C $160
D $180   **(2 marks)**

30 A company uses an overhead absorption rate of $3.50 per machine hour, based on 32,000 budgeted machine hours for the period. During the same period the actual total overhead expenditure amounted to $108,875 and 30,000 machine hours were recorded on actual production.

By how much was the total overhead under or over absorbed for the period?

A Under absorbed by $3,875
B Under absorbed by $7,000
C Over absorbed by $3,875
D Over absorbed by $7,000   **(2 marks)**

31 Which of the following statements relating to management information are true?

1. It is produced for parties external to the organisation
2. There is usually a legal requirement for the information to be produced
3. No strict rules govern the way in which the information is presented
4. It may be presented in monetary or non monetary terms

A 1 and 2
B 3 and 4
C 1 and 3
D 2 and 4   **(2 marks)**

32   A company's sales in the last year in its three different markets were as follows

	$
Market 1	100,000
Market 2	150,000
Market 3	50,000
Total	300,000

In a pie chart representing the proportion of sales made by each region what would be the angle of the section representing Market 3?

A   17 degrees
B   50 degrees
C   60 degrees
D   120 degrees   **(2 marks)**

33   Which of the following BEST describes a flexible budget?

A   A budget which shows variable production costs only

B   A monthly budget which is changed to reflect the number of days in the month

C   A budget which shows sales revenue and costs at different levels of activity

D   A budget that is updated halfway through the year to incorporate the actual results for the first
     half of the year   **(2 marks)**

34   The Eastland Postal Service is government owned. The government requires it to provide a parcel
      delivery service to every home and business in Eastland at a low price which is set by the government.
      Express Couriers Co is a privately owned parcel delivery company that also operates in Eastland. It is not
      subject to government regulation and most of its deliveries are to large businesses located in Eastland's
      capital city. You have been asked to assess the relative efficiency of the management of the two
      organisations.

      Which of the following factors should NOT be allowed for when comparing the ROCE of the two
      organisations to assess the efficiency of their management?

A   Differences in prices charged
B   Differences in objectives pursued
C   Differences in workforce motivation
D   Differences in geographic areas served   **(2 marks)**

35   Two products G and H are created from a joint process. G can be sold immediately after split-off. H
      requires further processing into product HH before it is in a saleable condition. There are no opening
      inventories and no work in progress of products G, H or HH. The following data are available for last
      period:

	$
Total joint production costs	350,000
Further processing costs of product H	66,000

Product	Production units	Closing inventory
G 4	20,000	20,000
HH	330,000	30,000

Using the physical unit method for apportioning joint production costs, what was the cost value of the
closing inventory of product HH for last period?

A $16,640
B $18,625
C $20,000
D $21,600   **(2 marks)**

36   Which TWO of the following are true for flexible budgets?

    (1)   A budget which is continually updated to reflect actual results
    (2)   A budget which has built in contingency to allow for unforeseen events
    (3)   A budget which identifies the cost behaviour of different cost items
    (4)   A budget which allows comparison of like with like

    A   1 and 2
    B   1 and 4
    C   2 and 3
    D   3 and 4   **(2 marks)**

37   A company manufactures and sells a single product. In two consecutive months the following levels of production and sales (in units) occurred:

	Month 1	Month 2
Sales	3,800	4,400
Production	3,900	4,200

The opening inventory for Month 1 was 400 units. Profits or losses have been calculated for each month using both absorption and marginal costing principles.

Which of the following combination of profits and losses for the two months is consistent with the above data?

	Absorption costing profit/(loss)		Marginal costing profit/(loss)	
	Month 1	Month 2	Month 1	Month 2
	$	$	$	$
A	200	4,400	(400)	3,200
B	(400)	4,400	200	3,200
C	200	3,200	(400)	4,400
D	(400)	3,200	200	4,400

    (2 marks)

38   A company wishes to evaluate a division which has the following extracts from income statement and statement of financial position.

Income statement:

	$'000
Sales	500
Gross profit	200
Net profit	120

Statement of financial position:

	$'000
Non current assets	750
Current assets	350
Current liabilities	(450)
Net assets	650

What is the residual income for the division if the company has a cost of capital of 18%?

    A $117,000
    B $21,600
    C $83,000
    D $3,000   **(2 marks)**

39 Under which of the following labour remuneration methods will direct labour cost always be a variable cost?

    A   Day rate
    B   Piece rate
    C   Differential piece rate
    D   Group bonus scheme   **(2 marks)**

40 A firm uses marginal costing. The following table shows the variances for a period when the actual net profit was $30,000.

Materials	$300 adverse
Labour	$800 favourable
Overheads	$550 adverse
Sales price variance	$400 favourable
Sales volume contribution variance	$800 favourable

What was the budgeted net profit for the period?

    A $28,850
    B $31,150
    C $30,050
    D $28,800   **(2 marks)**

41 The use of the balanced scorecard rather than a profit-based measure is likely to help solve the following problems:

    (1)   Subjectivity
    (2)   Short-termism

Which is/are true?

    A   1 only
    B   2 only
    C   Both 1 and 2
    D   Neither 1 nor 2   **(2 marks)**

42 A company operates a process in which no losses are incurred. The process account for last month, when there was no opening work-in-progress, was as follows:

Process Account

	$		$
Costs arising	624,000	Finished output (10,000 units)	480,000
		Closing work-in-progress (4,000 units)	144,000
	624,000		624,000

The closing work in progress was complete to the same degree for all elements of cost.

What was the percentage degree of completion of the closing work-in-progress?

    A   12%
    B   30%
    C   40%
    D   75%   **(2 marks)**

43   The purchase price of an item of inventory is $25 per unit. In each three month period the usage of the item is 20,000 units. The annual holding costs associated with one unit equate to 6% of its purchase price. The cost of placing an order for the item is $20.

What is the Economic Order Quantity (EOQ) for the inventory item to the nearest whole unit?

A   730
B   894
C   1,461
D   1,633   **(2 marks)**

44   A factory consists of two production cost centres (P and Q) and two service cost centres (X and Y). The total allocated and apportioned overhead for each is as follows:

P	Q	X	Y
$95,000	$82,000	$46,000	$30,000

It has been estimated that each service cost centre does work for other cost centres in the following proportions:

	P	Q	X	Y
Percentage of service cost centre X to	50	50	–	–
Percentage of service cost centre Y to	30	60	10	–

The reapportionment of service cost centre costs to other cost centres fully reflects the above proportions.

After the reapportionment of service cost centre costs has been carried out, what is the total overhead for production cost centre P?

A $124,500
B $126,100
C $127,000
D $128,500   **(2 marks)**

45   The following statements relate to responsibility centres:

(1)   Return on capital employed is a suitable measure of performance in both profit and investment centres.

(2)   Cost centres are found in manufacturing organisations but not in service organisations.

(3)   The manager of a revenue centre is responsible for both sales and costs in a part of an organisation.

Which of the statements, if any, is true?

A   1 only
B   2 only
C   3 only
D   None of them   **(2 marks)**

46   A company has recorded the following variances for a period:

Sales volume variance $10,000 adverse
Sales price variance $5,000 favourable
Total cost variance $12,000 adverse

Standard profit on actual sales for the period was $120,000.

What was the fixed budget profit for the period?

A $137,000
B $103,000
C $110,000
D $130,000   **(2 marks)**

47   A Company manufactures and sells one product which requires 8 kg of raw material in its manufacture. The budgeted data relating to the next period are as follows:

	Units
Sales	19,000
Opening inventory of finished goods	4,000
Closing inventory of finished goods	3,000

	Kg
Opening inventory of raw materials	50,000
Closing inventory of raw materials	53,000

What is the budgeted raw material purchases for next period (in kg)?

A   141,000
B   147,000
C   157,000
D   163,000   **(2 marks)**

48   The following statements relate to performance evaluation methods:

(1)   Residual income is not a relative measure
(2)   The return on investment figure is a relative measure
(3)   Residual income cannot be calculated for an individual project

Which of the above are correct?

A   1 and 2 only
B   1 and 3 only
C   2 and 3 only
D   1, 2 and 3   **(2 marks)**

49   A company has a budget for two products A and B as follows:

	Product A	Product B
Sales (units)	2,000	4,500
Production (units)	1,750	5,000
Skilled labour at $10/hour	2 hours/unit	2 hours/unit
Unskilled labour at $7/hour	3 hours/unit	4 hours/unit

What is the budgeted cost of unskilled labour for the period?

A $105,000
B $135,000
C $176,750
D $252,500   **(2 marks)**

50   Which TWO of the following are MOST likely to influence the motivation of budget holders?

(1)   The contents of the budget manual
(2)   The extent of participation in budget setting
(3)   The level of difficulty at which budgets are set
(4)   the structure of the budget committee

A   1 and 2
B   2 and 3
C   3 and 4
D   1 and 4   **(2 marks)**

(Total = 100 marks)

Answers to
Pilot Paper

Note: The ACCA examiner's answers can be found on page 189.

1   C   Functional benchmarking

2   A   Setting a cost by subtracting a desired profit margin from a competitive market price

3   C   F: normal loss = 65,000 × 8% = 5,200. Actual loss (65,000 – 58900) = 6,100

   G: normal loss = 37,500 × 5% = 1,875. Actual loss (37,500 – 35,700) = 1,800

   Therefore F shows an abnormal loss and G shows an abnormal gain

4   B   OAR = Budgeted overhead/budgeted production = $63,000/14,000 = $4.50 per unit

   Inventory has risen by 2,000 units so absorption costing will report a higher profit than marginal costing. 2,000 × $4.50 = $9,000

Absorption costing profit	$36,000
	$9,000
Marginal costing profit	$27,000

5   B

	$
53,000kg should have cost (× $2.50*)	132,500
But was	136,000
Material price variance	3,500(A)

   *Budgeted material cost per kg = $125,000/(25,000 units × 2kg)

6   B   Random sampling

7   C   2 and 3 only. A spreadsheet is not useful for storing large volumes of data. A database could perform this function

8   D   Graph D

9   B   Budgeting helps coordinate the activities of different departments and establishes a system of control

10   B   Participative budgeting increases the motivation of junior managers

11   A   Return on investment = Profit/capital employed

   Profit   = $36,000 + ($200,000 × 12%)

   = $60,000

   ROI   = $60,000/$200,000

   = 30%

12   C   An increase in material prices and an increase in raw material usage per unit could cause an adverse direct material variance

13   C   Variable cost per unit = (170,000 – 135,000 – 5,000)/(22,000 – 16,000) = $5

   Fixed cost = 135,000 – (16,000 × 5) = $55,000

   Total cost at 20,000 units:

   $55,000 + $5,000 + (20,000 × $5) = $160,000

14   A   Return on investment and market share

15   B   The correlation coefficient should be between -1 and 1.

16   C   Sales volume variance

17 A Use the high-low method to determine the fixed and variable elements

100	$15,120
60	$11,280
40	$3,840

$3,840/40 = $96 per %

Fixed element: $15,120 – (100 × 96) = $5,520

For 85% capacity, production cost would be 5,520 + (85 × $96) = $13,680

18 C $$IRR = A + \left[\frac{a}{a+b} \times (B - A)\right]$$

$$= 0.10 + \left[\frac{50}{50+30} \times (0.01)\right]$$

$$= 0.125$$

$$= 12.5\%$$

19 D A factor which limits the activities of an organisation

20 D A decrease in the ordering cost would reduce the EOQ (as smaller quantities could now be ordered) and also the holding cost (as lower inventories would be kept)

21 A

	$
Opening WIP	1,710
Completion of 300 units (300 × 40% × 10)	1,200
1,700 units @ $10	17,000
Total value 2,000 units	19,910

22 A

Budgeted hours	25,000
Actual hours	24,000
Capacity variance in hours	1,000 (A)
× standard fixed overhead absorption rate per hour*	×$5
	$5,000 (A)

*($125,000/25,000 = $5)

23 A Value analysis considers cost value, exchange value, use value and esteem value

24 A 1 and 2 only

25 B

Budgeted sales units	1,000
Actual sales units	900
Variance in units	100(A)
× budgeted profit ($50 – $39)	× $11
	$1,100(A)

26 B 1 and 2 only

27 A $$5,000 = x + \frac{x}{0.08} = 13.5x$$

Value of annual perpetuity = 5,000/13.5 = $370

28 C Quantified short term targets the organisation seeks to achieve

29 D Production in one standard hour = 20 units

Pay for 200 units = 200/20 × 18 = $180

This is above the guaranteed rate.

30   A

Overhead absorbed (30,000 × $3.5)	105,000
Actual overhead	108,875
Under-absorbed	3,875

31   B   No strict rules govern the way in which the information is presented. It may be presented in monetary or non-monetary terms.

32   C $\dfrac{50,000}{300,000} \times 360° = 60°$

33   C   A budget which shows sales revenue and costs at different levels of activity

34   C   Differences in workforce motivation

35   C

	$
Cost per unit joint production (350,000/ (420,000 + 330,000)	0.4666
Cost per unit further processing (66,000/330,000)	0.2
Total cost per unit	0.66666
Value of closing inventory (0.66666 x 30,000)	19,999

36   D   3 and 4

37   C   Closing inventory at the end of Month 1   = opening inventory + production – sales

38   D   RI   = controllable profit – imputed interest charge on controllable investment

= $120,000 – ($650,000 × 0.18)

= $3,000

39   B   Piece rate

40   A $30,000 + $300 – $800 + $550 – $400 – $800 = $28,850

41   B   It is likely to help prevent short-termism

42   D

Cost per unit of finished output (480,000/10,000)	$48
Cost per unit of work-in-progress (144,000/4,000)	$36

Therefore the WIP is 75% completed

43   C $EOQ = \sqrt{\dfrac{2CoD}{Ch}} = \sqrt{\dfrac{2 \times 20 \times (4 \times 20,000)}{25 \times 6\%}} = \sqrt{\dfrac{3,200,000}{1.5}} = 1,460.59$

44   D

	P	Q	X	Y
Total overhead	95,000	82,000	46,000	30,000
Reallocate Y	9,000	18,000	3,000	(30,000)
			49,000	
Reallocate X	24,500	24,500	(49,000)	
	128,500			

45   D   None of them

46   D   (Budgeted sales volume – actual sales volume) × standard profit per unit = $10,000 (A)

Standard profit on actual sales = (actual sales units × standard profit per unit) = $120,000

Fixed budget profit = $120,000 + $10,000 = $130,000

47	B	Production (units)	= Closing inventory + sales – opening inventory
			= 3,000 + 19,000 – 4,000
			= 18,000
		Raw material purchases	= Closing inventory + production – opening inventory
			= 53,000kg + (18,000 × 8kg) – 50,000kg
			= 147,000kg

48   A   1 and 2 only

49   C   (1,750 × 3 hours) + (5,000 × 4 hours) = 25,250 units

                   25,250 units × $7 = $176,750

50   B   2 and 3

ACCA examiner's answers to Pilot Paper

1   C

2   A

3   C

(litres)	Normal loss	Actual loss	Abnormal loss	Abnormal gain
Process F	5,200	6,100	900	–
Process G	1,875	1,800	–	75

4   B

Marginal costing profit:

(36,000 – (2,000*(63,000/14,000))

$27,000

5   B

Did cost:	$136,000
Should cost: (53,000 kg $2·50)	$132,500
Price variance:	$3,500

6   B

7   C

8   D

9   B

10 B

11 A   (36,000 + (200,000 x 12%))/200,000 = 30%

12 C

13 C

Using high low method:

Variable cost

(170,000 – 5,000 – 135,000)/(22,000 – 16,000) = $5

Fixed cost:

135,000 – (16,000*5) = 55,000

Cost for 20,000 units:

(20,000*5) + (55,000 + 5,000) = $160,000

14 A

15 B

16 C

17 A

Variable production cost per unit = (15,120 – 11,280)/(10,000– 6,000) = 3,840/4,000 = $0.96 Fixed cost = 11,280 – (6,000 × 0.96) = $5,520 85% capacity = 8,500 units. Flexible budget allowance for 8,500 units = $5,520 + (8,500 × 0.96) = $13,680

18 C

At 13% NPV should be –10

Using interpolation: 10% + (50/60)(10% – 13%) = 12.5%

19 D

20 D

21 A

1,700 units*10	$17,000
300 units*0.4*10	$1,200
Opening work in progress value	$1,710
Total value	$19,910

22 A

(Actual hours – Budgeted hours) * standard rate

(24,000 – 25,000)*5 = $5,000 adverse

23 A

24 A

25 B

(budgeted quantity – actual quantity) * standard profit per unit (1,000 – 900)*(50 – 39) = $1,100

26 B

27 A

5,000 = x + x/.08

5,000 = 13.5 x

Value of annual perpetuity = 5,000/13.5 = $370

28 C

29 D

200 units*(3/60)*18 = $180

30 A

Actual cost	$108,875
Absorbed cost	$105,000
Under absorbed	$3,875

31 B

32 C

Total number of degrees = 360

Proportion of market 3 sales: (50,000/300,000)*360 = 60

33 C

34 C

35 C

Joint costs apportioned to H: ((330,000/(420,000 + 330,000))*350,000 = $154,000
Closing inventory valuation(HH): (30,000/330,000)*(154,000 + 66,000) = $20,000

36 D

37 C

Month 1: production > sales   Absorption costing > marginal costing
Month 2: sales > production   marginal costing profit > absorption costing profit
A and C satisfy month 1, C and D satisfy month 2; therefore C satisfies both

38   D   ($120,000 – ($650,000*18%)) = $3,000

39   B

40   A   (30,000 + 300 – 800 + 550 – 400 – 800) = $28,850

41   B

42   D

Cost per equivalent unit (480,000/10,000) = $48

Degree of completion= ((144,000/48)/4,000) = 75%

43   C

$\{(2*20*(4*20,000))/(0\bullet06*25)\}^{0.5}$

1,461 units

44   D

Direct cost	$95,000
Proportion of cost centre X (46,000 + (0.10*30,000))*0.50	$24,500
Proportion of cost centre Y (30,000*0.3)	$9,000
Total overhead cost for P	$128,500

45   D

46   D

Sales volume variance:

(budgeted sales units – actual sales units) * standard profit per unit = 10,000 adverse

Standard profit on actual sales: (actual sales units * std profit per unit) = $120,000

Fixed budget profit: (120,000 + 10,000) = $130,000

47   B

Budgeted production (19,000 + 3,000 – 4,000) = 18,000 units

RM required for production (18,000*8) = 144,000 kg

RM purchases (144,000 + 53,000 – 50,000) = 147,000 kg

48   A

49   C   (($1,750*3 hrs) + ($5,000*4 hrs))*7 = $176,750

50   B

Mock Exam 2

FIA/ACCA
FMA/F2
Management Accounting

Mock Examination 2

Question Paper	
Time allowed	2 hours
ALL FIFTY questions are compulsory and MUST be answered	

DO NOT OPEN THIS PAPER UNTIL YOU ARE READY TO START UNDER EXAMINATION CONDITIONS

ALL 50 questions are compulsory and MUST be attempted

1   Three years ago the price index appropriate to Material Z had a value of 140. It now has a value of 180. The material costs $3,500 per kg today.

    What was its cost per kg three years ago?

    A $1,167
    B $2,722
    C $4,500
    D $6,222   **(2 marks)**

2   A government funded dentists offers free treatment to patients.

    What is the most likely principal budget factor?

    A   Labour hours
    B   Cash
    C   Demand
    D   Equipment   **(2 marks)**

3   A manufacturing company has four types of cost (identified as T1, T2, T3 and T4)

    The total cost for each type at two different production levels is:

Cost type	Total cost for 125 units	Total cost for 180 units
	$	$
T1	1,000	1,260
T2	1,750	2,520
T3	2,475	2,826
T4	3,225	4,644

    Which two cost types would be classified as being semi-variable?

    A   T1 and T3
    B   T1 and T4
    C   T2 and T3
    D   T2 and T4   **(2 marks)**

4   The operating statement used by an organisation to measure the performance of its divisions is structured as follows.

	$	$	$
External sales		X	
Internal transfers		X	
Variable cost of sales	(X)		
Other variable divisional costs	(X)		
		(X)	
Contribution		X	
Depreciation on controllable non current assets		(X)	
Other controllable fixed costs	(X)		
		(X)	
Controllable operating profit			X
Depreciation on other divisional non current assets		(X)	
Other traceable divisional costs	(X)		
		(X)	
Traceable divisional profit		X	
Apportioned head office cost		(X)	
Divisional net profit			X

    Which of the following would provide the best basis for measuring the performance of a manager of an investment centre?

    A   Divisional net profit
    B   Contribution
    C   Traceable divisional profit
    D   Controllable operating profit   **(2 marks)**

5   The performance of a publicly funded hospital is monitored using measures based upon the 'three Es'. The most important performance measure is considered to be the achievement of hospital targets for the successful treatment of patients.

Which of the three Es best describes this above measure?

A   Economy
B   Externality
C   Effectiveness
D   Efficiency   **(2 marks)**

6   An organisation is using linear regression analysis to establish an equation that shows a relationship between advertising expenditure and sales. It will then use the equation to predict sales for given levels of advertising expenditure. Data for the last five periods are as follows:

Period number	Advertising expenditure	Sales
	$'000	$'000
1	17	108
2	19	116
3	24	141
4	22	123
5	18	112

What are the values of 'Σx', 'Σy' and 'n' that need to be inserted into the appropriate formula?

	Σx	Σy	n
A	$600,000	$100,000	5
B	$100,000	$600,000	5
C	$600,000	$100,000	10
D	$100,000	$600,000	10

(2 marks)

7   Which of the following correlation coefficients indicates the weakest relationship between two variables?

A   + 1.0
B   + 0.4
C   − 0.6
D   − 1.0   **(2 marks)**

8   Which of the following statements are correct?

(i)   Strategic information is mainly used by senior management in an organisation
(ii)   Productivity measurements are examples of tactical information
(iii) Operational information is required frequently by its main users

A   (i) and (ii) only
B   (i) and (iii) only
C   (i), (ii) and (iii)   **(2 mark)**

9   A company manufactures two products P1 and P2 in a factory divided into two cost centres, X and Y. The following budgeted data are available:

	Cost centre	
	X	Y
Allocated and apportioned fixed overhead costs	$88,000	$96,000
Direct labour hours per unit:		
Product P1	3.0	1.0
Product P2	2.5	2.0

Budgeted output is 8,000 units of each product. Fixed overhead costs are absorbed on a direct labour hour basis.

What is the budgeted fixed overhead cost per unit for Product P2?

A $10
B $11
C $12
D $13   **(2 marks)**

10   A manufacturing company uses a machine hour rate to absorb production overheads, which were budgeted to be $130,500 for 9,000 machine hours. Actual overhead incurred were $128,480 and 8,800 machine hours were recorded.

What was the total under absorption of production overheads?

A $880
B $900
C $2,020
D $2,900   **(2 marks)**

11   A City Council uses a balanced scorecard approach to set objectives. The performance targets it has formulated are aimed at the following five objectives:

1   To improve reliability of the City bus services
2   To improve productivity of the tax-gathering department
3   To increase the number of tax-paying businesses and households in the city
4   To enhance the administration's management information systems
5   To increase the capacity of the City's refuse disposal service

Targets for these objectives have a customer perspective (C), a financial perspective (F), an internal process perspective (IP) or a learning and growth perspective (LG).

Which perspective will the performance target have for each of the five objectives listed above?

A   (IP) for objective 1, (F) for objective 2, (F) for objective 3, (LG) for objective 4 and (C) for objective 5
B   (IP) for objective 1, (IP) for objective 2, (F) for objective 3, (LG) for objective 4 and (C) for objective 5
C   (C) for objective 1, (LG) for objective 2, (IP) for objective 3, (IP) for objective 4 and (F) for objective 5
D   (C) for objective 1, (IP) for objective 2, (F) for objective 3, (LG) for objective 4 and (IP) for objective 5   **(2 marks)**

12   A company operates a job costing system. Job number 605 requires $300 of direct materials and $400 of direct labour. Direct labour is paid at the rate of $8 per hour. Production overheads are absorbed at a rate of $26 per direct labour hour and non-production overheads are absorbed at a rate of 120% of prime cost.

What is the total cost of job number 605?

A $2,000
B $2,400
C $2,840
D $4,400   **(2 marks)**

The following information relates to questions 13 and 14:

A company operates a process costing system using the first in first out (FIFO) method of valuation. No losses occur in the process.

The following date relate to last month:

	Units	Degree of completion	Value
Opening work in progress	100	60%	$680
Completed during the month	900		
Closing work in progress	150	48%	

The cost per equivalent unit of production for last month was $12.

13   What was the value of the closing work in progress?

A $816
B $864
C $936
D $1,800   (2 marks)

---

14   What was the total value of the units completed last month?

A $10,080
B $10,320
C $10,760
D $11,000   (2 marks)

---

15   A company's budgeted sales for last month were 10,000 units with a standard selling price of $20 per unit and a contribution to sales ratio of 40%. Last month actual sales of 10,500 units with total revenue of $204,750 were achieved.

What were the sales price and sales volume contribution variances?

	Sales price variance ($)	Sales volume contribution variance ($)
A	5,250 adverse	4,000 favourable
B	5,250 adverse	4,000 adverse
C	5,000 adverse	4,000 favourable
D	5,000 adverse	4,000 adverse
		(2 marks)

---

16   A company operates a standard absorption costing system. The standard fixed production overhead rate is $15 per hour.

The following data relate to last month: Actual hours worked	5,500
Budgeted hours	5,000
Standard hours for actual production	4,800

What was the fixed production overhead capacity variance?

A $7,500 adverse
B $7,500 favourable
C $10,500 adverse
D $10,500 favourable   (2 marks)

---

17   In the context of managing performance in 'not-for-profit' organisations, which of the following definitions is incorrect?

A   Efficiency means doing things quickly: minimising the amount of time that is spent on a given activity
B   Value for money means providing a service in a way which is economical, efficient and effective
C   Effectiveness means doing the right things: spending funds so as to achieve the organisation's objectives
D   Economy means doing things cheaply: not spending $2 when the same thing can be bought for $1   (2 marks)

18   A company purchased a machine several years ago for $50,000. Its written down value is now $10,000. The machine is no longer used on normal production work and it could be sold now for $8,000.

A one-off contract is being considered which would make use of this machine for six months. After this time the machine would be sold for $5,000.

What is the relevant cost of the machine to the contract?

    A $2,000
    B $3,000
    C $5,000
    D $10,000   **(2 marks)**

19   A company has monthly fixed costs of $10,000 and variable costs per unit of production of $15. The equation of the straight line relating productions (P) to costs (C) is:

    A $C = 10,000P + 15$
    B $P = 10,000 + 15C$
    C $C = 10,000 + 15/P$
    D $C = 10,000 + 15P$ **(2 marks)**

20   Which of the following make it difficult to measure performance in the service industry?

    1   Services are intangible
    2   A service is heterogeneous

    A   Both are true
    B   Both are false
    C   1 is true and 2 is false
    D   1 is false and 2 is true   **(2 marks)**

21   Which of the following statements best describe critical success factors?

    1   The financial ratios used by analysts to evaluate the organisation
    2   The personal objectives of the strategic management team
    3   Derived from the mission statement and objectives of the organisation
    4   The key areas that a business needs to succeed in, to ensure success overall

    A   1, 2, 3 and 4
    B   2 and 4 only
    C   1 and 3 only
    D   3 and 4 only   **(2 marks)**

22   Which of the following best describes tactical information?

    A   Mainly qualitative with some numerical analysis
    B   Sourced largely from external and informal sources
    C   Mainly quantitative, internal and generated frequently
    D   Based on operational information with some interpretation applied   **(2 marks)**

23   The table below contains details of an airline's expenditure on aviation fuel.

Year	Total expenditure on aviation fuel $ million	Total distance flown km million	Fuel price index
2008	600	4,200	120
2009	1,440	4,620	240

The following statements relate to the changes between 2008 and 2009.

1 The quantity of fuel consumed increased by 140%
2 The quantity of fuel consumed increased by 20%
3 The quantity of fuel consumed per km flown increased by 20%
4 The quantity of fuel consumed per km flown increased by 109%

Which statements are true?

A   1 only
B   2 only
C   2 and 3 only
D   2 and 4 only   (2 marks)

24   A company has two production departments and two service departments with the following fixed overheads:

	Production		Service	
	A	B	C	D
	$'000	$'000	$'000	$'000
	1,000	1,200	1,200	1,600

Service department C divides its time between the other departments in the ratio 3:2:1 (for A, B, and D respectively). Department D spends 40% of its time servicing Department A and 60% servicing Department B. If all service departments' overheads are allocated to production departments, the total fixed overhead cost of Department A is:

A $2,400,000
B $2,200,000
C $1,320,000
D $2,320,000   (2 marks)

25   An abnormal loss would arise when

(i)   Total losses are less than expected
(ii)   Total losses are greater than expected
(iii)   Total output is less than expected
(iv)   Total output is greater than expected

Which one of the following is correct?

A   (i) only
B   (i) and (ii)
C   (ii) and (iii)
D   (iii) and (iv)   (2 marks)

26   Up to a given level of activity in each period the purchase price per unit of a raw material is constant. After that point a lower price per unit applies both to further units purchased and also retrospectively to all units already purchased.

Which of the following graphs depicts the total cost of the raw materials for a period?

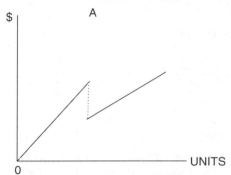

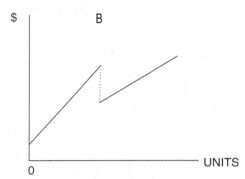

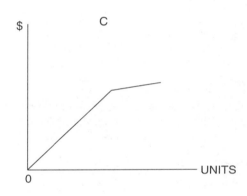

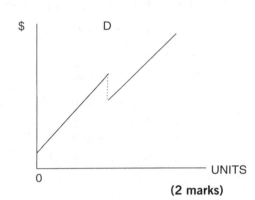

(2 marks)

27   An investment will produce an annual return of $1,500 in perpetuity with the first receipt starting in 3 years' time.

What is the present value of this perpetuity discounted at 6%?

A $21,000
B $22,250
C $25,000
D $25,250   **(2 marks)**

28   Organisations often have to make a trade-off between short-term and long-term objectives. Which of the following statements are correct?

1   Making short-term targets realistic can encourage a long-term view
2   Linking managers' rewards to share price may encourage a long-term view.

A   Both are true
B   Both are false
C   1 is true and 2 is false
D   1 is false and 2 is true   **(2 marks)**

29   An organisation has the following total costs at two activity levels:

Activity level (units)   17,000   22,000
Total costs ($)   140,000   170,000

Variable cost per unit is constant in this range of activity and there is a step up of $5,000 in the total fixed costs when activity exceeds 18,000 units.

What is the total cost at an activity level of 20,000 units?

A $155,000
B $158,000
C $160,000
D $163,000   (2 marks)

30   The following statements relate to financial accounting or to cost and management accounting:

(i)   The main users of financial accounting information are external to an organisation.
(ii)   Cost accounting is part of financial accounting and establishes costs incurred by an organisation.
(iii) Management accounting issued to aid planning, control and decision making.

Which of the statements are correct?

A   (i) and (ii) only
B   (i) and (iii) only
C   (ii) and (iii) only
D   (i), (ii) and (iii)   (2 marks)

31   An investment of $100,000 is made in a project. The scrap value is expected to be $15,000 at the end of the project. Four equal annual cash inflows of $35,000 will arise from the project, the first of which arises two years after the initial investment.

What is the payback period of the project?

A   2.3 years
B   2.9 years
C   3.3 years
D   3.9 years   (2 marks)

32   1   Simple payback period takes into account the time value of money and uses cash flows rather than profits.

      2   Internal rate of return takes into account the time value of money and uses cash flows rather than profits

Which of the above statements is/are true?

A   Statement 1 only
B   Statement 2 only
C   Statement 2 only
D   Statement 2 only   (2 marks)

33   A company uses 9,000 units of a component per annum. The component has a purchase price of $40 per unit and the cost of placing an order is $160. The annual holding cost of one component is equal to 8% of its purchase price.

What is the Economic Order Quantity (to the nearest unit) of the component?

A   530
B   671
C   949
D   1,342   (2 marks)

34 A bank pays a nominal 4.0% per annum with interest payable every six months

What is the effective annual rate of interest?

A 4.04%
B 4.16%
C 4.33%
D 8.16%   **(2 marks)**

35 Consider the following statements:

(i) Job costing is only applicable to service organisations.

(ii) Batch costing can be used when a number of identical products are manufactured together to go into finished inventory.

Is each statement TRUE or FALSE?

	Statement (i)	Statement (ii)
A	False	False
B	False	True
C	True	True
D	True	False

(2 marks)

36 An organisation absorbs overheads on a machine hour basis. The planned level of activity for last month was 30,000 machine hours with a total overhead cost of $247,500. Actual results showed that 28,000 machine hours were recorded with a total overhead cost of $238,000.

What was the total under absorption of overhead last month?

A $7,000
B $7,500
C $9,500
D $16,500   **(2 marks)**

37 The following information relates to a manufacturing company for next period:

	units		$
Production	14,000	Fixed production costs	63,000
Sales	12,000	Fixed selling costs	12,000

Using absorption costing for the profit for next period has been calculated as $36,000.

What would the profit for next period be using marginal costing?

A $25,000
B $27,000
C $45,000
D $47,000   **(2 marks)**

38 Information relating to two processes (F and G) was as follows:

Process	Normal loss as % of input	Input litres	Output litres
F	8	65,000	58,900
G	5	37,500	35,700

For each process, was there an abnormal loss or an abnormal gain?

	Profess F	Process G
A	Abnormal gain	Abnormal gain
B	Abnormal gain	Abnormal loss
C	Abnormal loss	Abnormal gain
D	Abnormal loss	Abnormal loss

(2 marks)

39   Last month 27,000 direct labour hours were worked at an actual cost of $236,385 and the standard direct labour hours of production were 29,880. The standard direct labour cost per hour was $8.50.

What was the labour efficiency variance?

A $17,595 Adverse
B $17,595 Favourable
C $24,480 Adverse
D $24,480 Favourable   (2 marks)

40   Last month a company's budgeted sales were 5,000 units. The standard selling price was $6 per unit with a standard contribution to sales ratio of 60%. Actual sales were 4,650 units with a total revenue $30,225.

What were the favourable sales price and adverse sales volume contribution variance?

	Sales price $	Sales volume contribution $
A	2,325	1,260
B	2,500	1,260
C	2,325	2,100
D	2,500	2,100

(2 marks)

41   The pharmacy in a busy hospital uses pre-determined rates for absorbing total overheads, based on the budgeted number of prescriptions to be handled. A rate of $7 per prescription has been calculated, and the following overhead expenditures have been estimated at two activity levels.

Total overheads $	Number of prescriptions
97,000	13,000
109,000	16,000

During a particular period fixed overheads were $45,000.

Based on the data above, what was the budgeted level of activity in prescriptions to be handled during the period in question?

A   13,000
B   15,000
C   16,000
D   33,333   (2 marks)

42   Which one of the following would be classified as indirect labour?

A   Assembly workers on a car production line
B   Bricklayers in a house building company
C   Forklift truck drivers in the stores of an engineering company
D   Tutors in a private education business   (2 marks)

43   The following statements relate to the calculation of the regression line $y = a + box$ using the information on the formulae sheet at the end of this examination paper:

(i)   n represents the number of pairs of data items used
(ii) $(\Sigma x)^2$ is calculated by multiplying Σx by Σx
(iii) Σxy is calculated by multiplying Σx by Σy

Which statements are correct?

A   (i) and (ii) only
B   (i) and (iii) only
C   (ii) and (iii) only
D   (i), (ii) and (iii)   (2 marks)

44   The correlation coefficient (r) for measuring the connection between two variables (x and y) has been calculated as 0.6.

How much of the variation in the dependent variable (y) is explained by the variation in the independent variable (x)?

A   36%
B   40%
C   60%
D   64%   **(2 marks)**

45   The following statements relate to relevant cost concepts in decision making:

(i)   Materials can never have an opportunity cost whereas labour can

(ii)   The annual depreciation charge is not a relevant cost

(iii) Fixed costs would have a relevant cost element if a decision causes a change in their total expenditure

Which statements are correct?

A   (i) and (ii) only
B   (i) and (iii) only
C   (ii) and (iii) only
D   (i), (ii) and (iii)   **(2 marks)**

46   In the last year a division's controllable return on investment was 25% and its controllable profit was $80,000. the cost of finance appropriate to the division was 18% per annum

What was the division's controllable residual income in the last year?

A $5,600
B $22,400
C $74,400
D $76,400   **(2 marks)**

47   In a process where there are no work–in–progress inventories, two joint products (J and K) are created. Information (in units) relating to last month is as follows:

Product	Sales	Opening inventory of finished goods	Closing inventory of finished goods
J	6,000	100	300
K	4,000	400	200

Joint production costs last month were $110,000 and these were apportioned to joint products based on the number of units produced.

What were the joint production costs apportioned to product J for last month?

A $63,800
B $64,000
C $66,000
D $68,200   **(2 marks)**

48   Four years ago material X cost $5 per kg and the price index most appropriate to the cost of material X stood at 150. The same index now stands at 430.

What is the best estimate of the current cost of material X per kg?

A $1.74
B $9.33
C $14.33
D $21.50   **(2 marks)**

The following information relates to questions 49 and 50.

A company has established the following selling price, costs and revenue equations for one of its products:

Selling price ($ per unit) = 50 – 0.025Q

Marginal revenue ($ per unit) = 50 – 0.05Q

Total costs per month ($) = 2,000 + 15Q

Q represents the number of units produced and sold per month.

49   At what selling price will monthly profits be maximised?

     A $15.00
     B $17.50
     C $25.00
     D $32.50   **(2 marks)**

50   What would be the monthly profit if the selling price per unit was set at $20?

     A $1,000
     B $4,000
     C $6,000
     D $12,000   **(2 marks)**

(Total = 100 marks)

Answers to
Mock Exam 2

1 B $\$3,500 \times \dfrac{140}{180} = \$2,722$

2 B Cash

3 A

Cost type	Total cost for 125 units	Cost per unit @ 125 units	Total cost for 180 units	Cost per unit @ 180 units
	$	$	$	$
T1	1,000	8.00	1,260	7.00
T2	1,750	14.00	2,520	14.00
T3	2,475	19.80	2,826	13.75
T4	3,225	25.80	4,644	25.80

Cost types T1 and T3 have different costs per unit at different activity levels and are therefore most likely to be classified as semi-variable costs.

Cost types T2 and T4 have the same cost per unit at different levels of activity and are therefore wholly variable costs.

4 D Controllable operating profit

5 C Effectiveness

6 B

Period number	Advertising expenditure $'000	Sales $'000
1	17	108
2	19	116
3	24	141
4	22	123
5	18	112
	100	600

N = 5 (five pairs of data)

Sales (y) are dependent on the levels of advertising expenditure (x).

7 B + 0.4 indicates the weakest relationship between two variables.

8 C Statements (i), (ii) and (iii) are all correct.

9 D

	Cost centre	
	x	y
	$	$
Overheads	88,000	96,000

Budgeted direct labour hours		
Product P1	24,000 hours	8,000 hours
Product P2	20,000 hours	16,000 hours
	44,000 hours	24,000 hours

Budgeted overhead absorption rate

Cost centre X = $\dfrac{\$88,000}{44,000\,hours}$ = $2 per direct labour hour

Cost centre Y = $\dfrac{\$96,000}{24,000\,hours}$ = $4 per direct labour hour

Budgeted fixed overhead cost per unit – Product P2
Cost centre x = 2.5 hours $2 per direct labour hour
= $5
Cost centre y = 2 hours @ $4 per direct labour hour
= $8
∴ fixed overhead per unit of Product P2 = $(5+8)
= $13

10   A

	$
Overhead absorbed (8,800 machine hours × $14.50*)	127,600
Actual overhead	128,480
Under-absorbed overhead	880

* Budgeted overhead absorption rate = $\dfrac{\$130,500}{9,000\,\text{machine hours}}$ = $14.50 per machine hour

11   D   A target for improving the reliability of the City bus service (objective 1) is primarily an issue of service quality, and has a customer objective. Improving productivity and capacity of services (objectives 2 and 5) have an internal process perspective. Increasing the number of tax-payers (objective 3) is a financial objective. Improving management information systems (objective 4) has an information and learning perspective.

12   C   Total cost – job number 605

	$
Direct materials	300
Direct labour	400
Prime cost	700
Production overheads ($26 × $400/$8)	1,300
	2,000
Non-production overheads (120% × $700)	840
Total cost – job number 605	2,840

13   B   Closing work in progress   = 48% × 150 units × $12

= $864

14   C

	$
Opening work in progress	680
Completed in month (800* × $12)	9,600
Opening work in progress (40 × $12)	480
Total value of units completed	10,760

* 900 units – 100 units = 800 units

15   A

	$
Sales revenue from 10,500 units should have been × $20)	210,000
but was	204,750
Sales price variance	5,250 (A)

$\dfrac{\text{contribution per unit}}{\$20} = 0.4$

∴ contribution per unit = 0.4 × $20

= $8

Budgeted sales	10,000 units
Actual sales	10,500 units
Sales volume variance	500 units (F)
× standard contribution per unit	× $8
Sales volume contribution variance	$4,000 (F)

16   B

Budgeted hours of work	5,000 hours
Actual hours of work	5,500 hours
Fixed production overhead capacity variance	500 hours (F)
× standard fixed production overhead rate	× $15
Fixed production overhead capacity variance (in $)	7,500 (F)

17   A   Efficiency does not mean doing things quickly. It means doing things well and getting the best use out of the money spent. Efficiency can be measured as the input/output ratio for any process or activity. All other definitions are correct for a not-for-profit organisation.

18   B

	$
Sales proceeds now	8,000
Sales proceeds – six months	5,000
Relevant cost of machine	3,000

19   D   C = 10,000 + 15P

20   A   Both are true. Intangible means that the actual benefit being bought can not be touched. This can make it difficult to inspect, for example, the quality of the service. A service is heterogeneous. The service received will vary each time. Services are more reliant on people. People are not robots, so how the service is delivered will not be identical each time.This can also make performance measurement difficult.

21   D   By monitoring the critical success factors, management ensure that they are on track to succeed in their mission and objectives. The personal objectives of the strategic management team should mirror the critical success factors of the organisation, but are likely to contain personal objectives such as individual development targets. The CSFs may contain some of the financial ratios used by analysts to evaluate the organisation but there will be other qualitative factors as well. The CSFs should drive the information requirements of the organisation – not the other way round.

22   D   Tactical information is medium term and drawn largely from internal/operational sources. It is the job of middle management to analyse it further in order to use it for decision making. Quantitative information that is generated frequently is normally found at the operational level and qualitative information from a range of sources will be found more at the strategic level.

23   B $1,440 \times \dfrac{120}{240} = 720$

$\dfrac{720}{600} = 1.2 = 120\%$ so the increase is 20%

24   D

	A	B	C	D
	$'000	$'000	$'000	$'000
Fixed overheads	1,000	1,200	1,200	1,600
C (3:2:1)	600	400	(1,200)	200
				1,800
D (40:60)	720	1,080		(1,800)
	2,320			

25   C   (ii)   If more losses have been incurred than expected, the loss is abnormally high.
              (iii)   If output is less than expected, losses must be higher than expected.

26   A   Graph A

27   B   Value of income one year before first receipt is due:

$1,500/0.06 = $25,000

Discounting back to today using a discount factor of 6% over 2 years:

PV   = $25,000 x 0.890

       = $22,250

28   A   Both are true. If budget targets are unrealistically tough, a manager will be forced to make trade-offs between the short and long term. Linking managers' rewards to share price may encourage goal congruence.

29   C   Variable cost per unit $= \dfrac{(170,000 - 5,000) - 140,000}{22,000 - 17,000}$

$= \$5$

At 22,000 units, fixed costs $= \$170,000 - (22,000 \times \$5)$
$= \$60,000$

Total cost at an activity level of 20,000 units $= \$60,000 + (20,000 \times \$5)$
$= \$160,000$

30   B   Cost accounting is not part of financial accounting.

31   D

Time	Cashflow ($)	Cumulative cash flow ($)
0	(100,000)	(100,000)
2	35,000	(65,000)
3	35,000	(30,000)
4	35,000	5,000

Payback is therefore 3 years and (30,000/35,000) = 3.9 years

32   B   Only statement 2 is true.

33   C $EOQ = \sqrt{2 \times C_o \times D / C_h}$

$C_o = \$160$
$D = 9,000$ units
$C_h = 8\% \times \$40 = \$3.20$

$EOQ = \sqrt{2 \times 160 \times 9,000 / 3.2}$

$= 949$ units

34   A $[(1.02^2 - 1) \times 100]$

35   B   Job costing can also be used in manufacturing organisations.

36   A   Overhead absorption rate = $247,500/30,000 = $8.25
Absorbed overheads = 28,000 × $8.25 = $231,000
Actual cost = $238,000
Under absorption = 238,000 – 231,000 = $7,000

37   B   The fixed overhead absorbed into the inventory valuation is the difference in the marginal costing profit.

Inventory = 14,000 – 12,000 = 2,000 units

Value of fixed production costs absorbed into inventory

= 2,000 × 63,000/14,000

= $9,000

Marginal costing profit = 36,000 – 9,000 = $27,000

38   C   Process F: Expected output = 92% × 65,000 = 59,800 litres

Actual output = 58,900 litres

There is an abnormal loss

Process G: Expected output = 95% × 37,500 = 35,625 litres

Actual output = 35,700 litres

There is an abnormal gain

39   D

Actual hours @ standard rate	27,000 × $8.50 = $299,500
Standard hours @ standard rate	29,880 × $8.50 = $253,980
Labour efficiency variance	$24,480 F

40   A   Sales price variance:

              Actual sales @ standard rate $4,650 \times \$6 = \$27,900$

              Standard sales at actual price $= \$30,225$

              Labour efficiency variance $\underline{\$2,325}$ F

              Sales volume contribution variance:

              Standard contribution = $\$6 \times 60\% = \$3.60$ per unit

              Volume variance = 5,000 – 4,650 = 350 units A

              @ \$3.60   = \$1,260 A

41   B   15,000

              Variable overhead + fixed overhead = total overhead

              ∴ Fixed overhead per prescription = \$7 – \$4 = \$3

              Total fixed overheads   = \$45,000

              ∴ Budgeted activity level $= \dfrac{\$45,000}{\$3} = 15,000$ prescriptions

42   C   The drivers are not working directly on engineering projects

43   A Σxy is calculated by multiplying x and y for each data item and then adding all of the results.

44   A   The variation is given by the coefficent of determination, r^2

              $r^2 = 0.6 \times 0.6 = 0.36$

45   C   Materials can have an opportunity cost if they could have been used for something else.

46   B $\$80,000 - (\$80,000 \div 0.25 \times 0.18)$

47   D   Production in units:

              J: 6,000 – 100 + 300 =   6,200

              K: 4,000 – 400 + 200 =   <u>3,800</u>

                                                  <u>10,000</u>

              Joint costs apportioned to J:

              6,200/10,000 x \$110,000 = \$68,200

48   C   (\$5 X 430) ÷ 150.

49   D   Profits are maximised when marginal revenue = marginal cost

              Marginal revenue = 50 – 0.05Q

              Marginal cost = 15

              50 – 0.05Q = 15

              $Q = \dfrac{50 - 15}{0.05}$

              Q = 700

              Selling price = 50 – 0.025Q

                              = 50 – (0.025 × 700)

                              = \$32.50

50   B   When selling price is $20:

20 = 50 − 0.025Q

$$Q = \frac{50 - 20}{0.025}$$

= 1,200

At 1,200 units:

Total revenue = 1,200 × $20 = $24,000

Total costs   = 2,000 + (15 × 1,200) = $20,000

Profit   = 24,000 − 20,000 = $4,000

REVIEW FORM

Name: _____   Address: _____

_____

Date:_____   _____

How have you used this Practice & Revision Kit?
(Tick one box only)

☐ Distance learning (book only)

☐ On a course: college _____

☐ As a tutor

☐ With 'correspondence' package

☐ Other _____

Why did you decide to purchase this Practice & Revision Kit? *(Tick one box only)*

☐ Have used complementary Interactive Text

☐ Have used BPP Texts in the past

☐ Recommendation by friend/colleague

☐ Recommendation by a lecturer at college

☐ Saw advertising

☐ Other _____

☐ Our advertisement in *ACCA Student Accountant*

☐ Our advertisement in *Teach Accounting*

☐ Other advertisement

☐ Our brochure with a letter through the post

☐ ACCA E-Gain email

☐ BPP email

☐ Our website www.bpp.com

Which (if any) aspects of our advertising do you find useful?
(Tick as many boxes as are relevant)

☐ Prices and publication dates of new editions

☐ Information on Practice & Revision Kit content

☐ Facility to order books off-the-page

☐ None of the above

During the past six months do you recall seeing/receiving any of the following?
(Tick as many boxes as are relevant)

Have you used the companion Interactive Text for this subject?   ☐ Yes ☐ No

Your ratings, comments and suggestions would be appreciated on the following areas

	Very useful	Useful	Not useful
Introductory section (How to use this Practice & Revision Kit)	☐	☐	☐
'Do You Know' checklists	☐	☐	☐
'Did You Know' checklists	☐	☐	☐
Possible pitfalls	☐	☐	☐
Questions	☐	☐	☐
Answers	☐	☐	☐
Mock exams	☐	☐	☐
Structure & presentation	☐	☐	☐
Icons	☐	☐	☐

	Excellent	Good	Adequate	Poor
Overall opinion of this Kit	☐	☐	☐	☐

Do you intend to continue using BPP Interactive Texts/Kits?   ☐ Yes ☐ No

Please note any further comments and suggestions/errors on the reverse of this page.

Please return to: Ian Blackmore, BPP Learning Media Ltd, FREEPOST, London, W12 8BR

REVIEW FORM (continued)

Please note any further comments and suggestions/errors below